Online learning
and
social exclusion

Online learning and social exclusion

Alan Clarke

niace

promoting adult learning

Published by the National Institute of Adult Continuing Education
(England and Wales)

Renaissance House
20 Princess Road West
Leicester
LE1 6TP

Company registration no. 2603322
Charity registration no. 1002775

First published 2002, reprinted 2003

promoting adult learning

NIACE, the national organisation for adult learning, has a broad remit to
promote lifelong learning opportunities for adults.
NIACE works to develop increased participation in education
and training. It aims to do this for those who do not have easy access because
of barriers of class, gender, age, race, language and culture, learning
difficulties or disabilities, or insufficient financial resources.

Cataloguing in Publication Data
A CIP record of this title is available from the British Library

ISBN   1 86201 115 X

Designed and typeset by Prestige Filmsetters, Leicester, UK
Printed and bound in Great Britain by Alden Press

Acknowledgements

I would like to thank my colleagues at NIACE for their support and assistance, in particular Alan Tuckett, Alice McLure, Andy Kail, Cheryl Turner, Ewa Rawicka, Fiona Aldridge, Helen Biggs, Jackie Essom, Keith Lindsay, Lisa Englebright, Munira Abdulhusein and Peter Lavender.

Contents

1   Executive summary   1
2   Introduction   5
3   Nature of social exclusion and learning   8
4   Trends in technology and learning   11
5   What is online learning?   13
6   Online learning issues   15
    6.1   Online learners   18
    6.2   Tutorial support   21
    6.3   Other forms of support   24
    6.4   Wider participation   26
    6.5   Collaborative learning   28
    6.6   Vicarious learning   32
    6.7   Design of materials   34
    6.8   Learning to learn   37
    6.9   Characteristics of different approaches   39
    6.10 Moderating and facilitating   42
    6.11 Location of access   45
    6.12 Costs and benefits   48
    6.13 Retention   50

7   Social issues   52
    7.1   Socially-excluded communities   53
    7.2   Access to and use of the internet   55
    7.3   Learners' attitudes   59
    7.4   Online communities   65
    7.5   Informal learning   68
    7.6   Teleworking   70
    7.7   Digital democracy   72
    7.8   Access to knowledge   74
    7.9   Barriers to online learning   75
    7.10 ICT and the family   77
    7.11 ICT in the community   81
    7.12 ICT and the learner   85
    7.13 ICT in the organisation   87

8   Conclusions and recommendations   89
9   References   91

Tables and figures

Tables

Table 1 Comparing traditional and online collaborative learning — 29

Table 2 Comparing learning organisation objectives and communication technologies — 41

Table 3 Use of the home computer — 56

Table 4 Participation in learning and future intention to learn, by access to the internet — 58

Table 5 Awareness and perceived usefulness of new technologies — 60

Table 6 Personal perceived usefulness of personal computers — 61

Table 7 Perceived usefulness of the internet — 61

Table 8 Informal learning and the internet — 69

Table 9 Potential for teleworking — 71

Figures

Figure 1 Overall laptop use — 82

Figure 2 Location of use — 83

Figure 3 Who are the learners? — 83

1 *Executive summary*

Online learning

Online learning covers a wide range of technologies and learning methods including both formal (e.g. online courses) and informal (e.g. surfing the internet) learning. There is significant interest and enthusiasm for online learning across all education and training sectors. A key factor for this enthusiasm is that it has the potential to overcome many of the barriers that socially- and economically-disadvantaged adults face in accessing learning opportunities, in particular those of place, pace and time. This potential will not be realised simply by access alone. It requires many different and inter-related actions to be taken. In particular it needs structures in place to support and encourage participation.

Many excluded adults have had poor experiences of formal education and so are unconvinced of the relevance of learning to themselves. This is compounded by the fact that many of them have major doubts about the value of information and communication technologies (ICT) to their lives and are often apprehensive about technology. This may take the form of doubt about their own ability to learn how to use ICT. There is some evidence of a positive attitude towards online learning in general, although this may be due to it being perceived as new and exciting.

In order to take part in online learning, people need to have access to the technology combined with competence and confidence in using ICT. Many socially-disadvantaged adults neither use technology nor are interested in it. There is a major challenge to providers of ICT learning in attracting the many people who do not see the relevance of ICT to their lives. The digital or information divide already exists in British society. The use of and access to ICT is related to age, geography, gender, income and educational attainment.

Online learning is a form of open learning. Open learning has been studied extensively in Britain. The stereotypical successful open learner is motivated, mature and confident, with a history of educational achievement (Simpson, 2000). Neverthless, there are examples of learners with no recent educational experience and with limited self-confidence who have succeeded with open learning (Crowley-Bainton, 1995). This was achieved by systematically planning to provide the best materials and the most appropriate support. It did not come about by accident.

Support

Personal support is vital to online learning. It needs to be provided before and during all stages of the learning process and in many different ways. A major weakness with all forms of open learning is retention, which appears to be related to previous educational achievement. Adults who are returning to learning after a poor initial experience are the most vulnerable. This is compounded by the same adults probably having the least confidence and experience with using ICT and possibly the most under-developed learning skills. There is a major risk that online learning will fail many of these learners unless support structures are effective.

Access

Many adults have significant problems simply attending and taking part in traditional forms of learning and although technology is not a solution to all problems, it can assist in overcoming some of physical barriers to participating. However, there is a clear lack of understanding and knowledge of these technical solutions amongst practitioners.

Collaborative learning

Open and distance learning is frequently associated with individual or even isolated learning. Considerable research and development has been undertaken in the field of collaborative online learning, which is learning and working in a group separated by distance but brought together by communication technology. This has the potential to provide a powerful learning experience. However, most of the research and development has been undertaken within a context other than adults returning to learning so it is not clear how much of the information can be transferred into more complex and challenging circumstances.

Learning materials

It is widely accepted that the current availability of high quality online learning materials is very limited. This is partially due to the rapid development of these methods, resulting in limited experience of designing suitable learning materials combined with relatively few trained and experienced computer-based learning designers.

Cost

A critical factor in producing any form of computer-based learning material is the high initial cost of producing good quality material. This is likely to prove a barrier to new organisations entering the market and limiting the volume of materials.

Learning skills

Using ICT to deliver and support learning requires learners to have appropriate learning skills. In many cases we are assuming that learners are studying on their own, with their peers and tutors only available through communication links. It is unlikely that adults returning to learning after many years or with poor previous experience of education will have developed these learning skills. A key element in online learning is likely to be the development of learning skills.

Location

One of the main benefits of online learning is that it can provide access to learning at an appropriate place (e.g. home, learning centre and the work place). Each location will have both advantages and disadvantages to the learner, none of them being perfect. All require a combination of support and course design changes that will tailor the learning content to the particular environment.

Disadvantage

Adults who are socially excluded experience many different forms of disadvantage. Online learning is not going to overcome all or even the majority of these factors. In order for online learning to fulfil its potential, the needs of disadvantaged individuals and communities must be carefully considered and the use of online methods tailored to meet these needs. They must be integrated into other initiatives to develop the community and its people.

Online communities

ICT provides the means of creating online communities. These can take many forms and are not limited by geography or time. It is possible for people in all parts of the world to communicate as easily as if they lived in the same street. In a similar way, communication is not limited by being in the same time zone. Messages can be sent at any time and read whenever it is convenient to the individual. Online communities are communities of shared interest or characteristics (e.g. age, hobby, health, shared experience, occupation or problems). Families scattered around the world can maintain their links through email as if they still lived in the same house. Ethnic minorities can maintain their language and culture by connecting with each other and to online newspapers.

Informal Learning

One model of online learning is based on the consideration that the internet is a gigantic library of information through which you can surf, finding the information and knowledge you need. This type of informal learning has the potential to reach many adults who have had poor experience of formal education and are reluctant to return to a course of study in an institutional setting. However, it does assume learners are confident ICT users and are competent in searching for and judging the quality of information. These are advanced skills that a person returning to learning or new to the internet is unlikely to possess.

Teleworking

Teleworking is growing rapidly on both a full- and part-time basis. It is very different from the traditional forms of home working but is attractive for similar reasons, that is, teleworking allows you to work within the constraints of family and other factors. It does assume that you are a competent ICT user and have access to ICT in your home. At the moment, teleworking opportunities tend to be provided to existing employees who have skills and experience that the organisation values. That said, teleworking is still being developed so wider opportunities may become available.

Democracy

The development of online Government information and services, access to Members of Parliament by email, the trend towards online shopping and the creation of the 'information society' are leaving adults without ICT skills and access at a serious disadvantage. As society migrates to the online world it is likely that socially-excluded groups will be further disadvantaged.

Learning opportunities

The Adult and Community Learning laptop initiative has shown that ICT can provide a wide range of learning opportunities (e.g. basic skills, art, technology and self-confidence) to many different groups of learners (e.g. unemployed people, ethnic minorities, older learners and young people) in almost any community location.

Organisations

Current access to online learning in organisations is following the traditional pattern of access to training. Managers have considerably more training opportunities than other staff and this is mirrored by access to ICT. Online learning so far has not helped to address social and economic disadvantage within employment.

Conclusion

Although there is a great deal of activity in relation to online learning, it is clear that there are many gaps in our understanding of how to realise its potential. The evidence is skewed and relatively little research has been undertaken in the community context. Implementation is proceeding far faster than investigation. It is therefore critical that developments are accompanied by evaluation and dissemination to ensure that practitioners have access to the latest information.

2 *Introduction*

Online learning has the potential to contribute to removing some of the barriers which people who are socially- or economically-disadvantaged face when accessing learning opportunities. Online learning can provide learning opportunities:

▶ at locations acceptable to disadvantaged people (e.g. community centres, schools, village halls and homes)
▶ at a pace which the individual learner can adjust to meet their preferences
▶ at a time which meets the needs and family responsibilities of learners
▶ which normally would not be available or suitable.

All the same, online learning is a relatively new development with research and other evidence only partially available. A great deal of the evidence is based on the experience of universities delivering learning to students in higher education. How much of this is transferable to the delivery of learning to socially-disadvantaged people is difficult to assess. For adults to use online learning requires both physical access to the technology and the skills, and the knowledge and understanding to enable them to be confident users of it.

Access to the internet is growing rapidly (National Statistics, 2000) with about 32 per cent of households in England with an internet link. There are many initiatives to extend access to ICT (information and communication technologies) including 1000 Learndirect learning centres, 6000 UK Online centres (although this will include many in other categories), every further education college, every library (People's Network) and other local Government initiatives, as well as cybercafes and telecottages. This is significant access. However, access is not enough since many people lack confidence, do not see the relevance or are simply unaware of the possibilities of ICT. The National Statistics results show that households with internet connections varied according to geographical locations (e.g. 25% in London but only 11% in Northern Ireland), income (e.g. 48% of highest earners but only 6% of lowest) and family structure (e.g. more access to families with children). Headline figures often disguise the underlying patterns of ownership and competence in ICT that have been shown to be related to gender, income, age and educational attainment. Fundamentally, if you are socially disadvantaged then you are less likely to have access to or have the opportunity to become a competent user of ICT.

Access to ICT needs to be combined with encouragement and support mechanisms to bring people into community learning centres, libraries or other locations. ICT needs to be combined with and integrated into other community development processes and actions. This requires the employment of outreach methods.

BISHOP BURTON COLLEGE

Taking part in online learning requires learners who are confident and competent users of ICT so that it is an aid to their learning and not another barrier to be overcome. Current ICT introductory courses tend to concentrate on particular applications rather than developing underpinning and transferable skills and knowledge. If graduates of these courses do not progress to more advanced ones or have opportunities to practise then it is likely their new skills will rapidly fade. The demand for basic and introductory courses is massive and growing, with approximately 400,000 adults undertaking basic ICT qualifications each year.

A key part of the ICT market is the continuing high rate of change, with the constant emergence of new products and upgrading of old ones. It has been estimated that 60 per cent of software is less than 2 years old and that the mean shelf life of technical skills is only 2 years (OECD, 1996; GHK Economics and Management, 1998). These changes often reflect the market position of producers rather than the technical superiority of the products so that it is difficult to predict trends. It is widely accepted that one of the few characteristics of ICT that is predictable is its unpredictability. This pace of change and the unpredictable nature of ICT means that to remain a competent ICT user requires a continuous effort to maintain skills and knowledge.

Within further and higher education ICT has made a significant impact on both teaching staff and learners. ICT has been used in a wide range of ways. The main ways are:

▶ the availability of computers to provide access for staff and learners to software applications such as word processors to prepare handouts and write assignments
▶ the use of communication technology (e.g. email, mailgroups and bulletin boards) to assist learners and staff to support each other
▶ college websites which are able to provide up-to-date information
▶ developing learning centres
▶ developing learning materials
▶ delivering learning materials (e.g. courseware, online interactive learning resources and downloadable materials).

The scale and balance of the use of technology in learning is skewed, with straightforward use of computer applications probably being most significant. However the use of email to communicate between teachers and learners is now widespread. Learning centres are available in many colleges and universities although their role varies from simply providing access to computer technology to centres specialising in supporting specific learning issues (e.g. numeracy centres). However the use of interactive learning material is still relatively limited perhaps due to the availability of quality products and designers in further and higher education to develop in-house materials. There is considerable interest and development underway to produce interactive learning materials so that this availability is likely to significantly increase.

Online learning is also growing rapidly within organisations with many major employers making substantial investments in materials and facilities (Epic Group, 2000). This appears to be mainly focused on large organisations and does not include small- and medium-sized enterprises. However these are a priority for Learndirect services and many ADAPT/Ufi development projects have concentrated on them.

In all sectors of the economy online learning is being discussed with considerable enthusiasm, yet it is not always apparent how much is simple rhetoric and how much is action.

Key conclusion

▶ Online learning has the potential to overcome many of the barriers which socially- and economically-disadvantaged adults face. To realise this potential requires sustained action.

3 Nature of social exclusion and learning

Reluctance to take part

Many adults who are socially- or economically-disadvantaged have had poor experiences of formal education so that they are often unwilling or reluctant to take part in courses in institutional settings. The Policy Action Team's report on skills (2000) stated that the national education and training system was not addressing the needs of socially-disadvantaged people with many adults feeling they had nothing to gain. Many disadvantaged adults are unconvinced of the relevance of learning to their lives. They are likely to lack confidence in their own abilities to succeed at learning. These are general statements of disadvantage while specific problems of access also apply, such as:

- the high cost of public transport
- rural isolation or timetabling
- family responsibilities which limit availability and opportunities (e.g. lone parents and carers)
- disability
- the expense of the course.

A comparison of the participation in learning by socio-economic class from 1990-2000 shows that there has been little change and class is a key predictor of participation. Fifty-eight per cent of socio-class AB are current or recent learners compared to only 36 per cent of skilled (C2) and 25 per cent of unskilled working class (DE). Thirty-nine per cent of skilled and 57 per cent of unskilled working class have undertaken no learning since leaving school (Sargant, 2000). Sargant showed that past success in learning led directly to future intentions. Seventy-five per cent of current learners intended to study more in the next 3 years, while 87 per cent of people who have undertaken no learning since leaving school are unlikely to take part in learning in the future.

ICT encouraging learning

This is the context in which the potential of online learning needs to be delivered. Clarke (1998) reports that relatively short ICT (informantion and communication technologies) tasters for disadvantaged adults are often enough to encourage them to undertake further study. *Pathways in Adult Learning* (DfEE, 1999) confirmed that a short episode of learning could lead to participation in longer programmes of study.

Modern technology is frequently reported as interesting adults and perhaps motivating them to take part in events while other subjects would not. The Basic Skills Agency (2000), reporting on a MORI interview survey, suggest that 50 per cent of adults would be motivated to improve their basic skills if it involved learning on a computer and 49 per cent if it could be combined with improving their computer skills. A wide range of other surveys has shown a significant interest in learning about ICT (NOP, 1997; Future.com, 1997; and Sargant *et al.*, 1997).

Learning about and through ICT is clearly motivating for many adults. Nevertheless, many adults do not see the relevance of ICT to their lives and this group appears to be composed of people who would also be unlikely to take part in learning. It is therefore far from straightforward to assume that simply making online learning available will bring about a significant increase in participation. To help people access technology and support them in taking advantage of online learning will require a combination of outreach activities, mentoring and tutorial support adapted to meet the context of online learning (McGivney, 2000; Wood, 2000; Clarke, 1998). The current position in general is that staff with online learning skills and experience have little experience of outreach, mentoring and support in community settings. Equally staff with experience of delivering learning in the community have little understanding of online learning and perhaps ICT in general.

The issues

The Policy Action Team's report (2000) stated that the education and training system:

▶ provided few opportunities to develop generic skills (e.g. self-confidence)
▶ provided a complex and confusing qualification system
▶ did not treat the needs as priorities
▶ provided poor collaboration in planning provision
▶ provided limited first steps provision
▶ offered provision which was difficult to access.

The National Skills Task Force (2000) identified the following as priorities for the economy:

▶ basic skills
▶ generic skills
▶ mathematics skills
▶ intermediate level skills
▶ ICT skills
▶ management and leadership skills.

A New Commitment to Neighbourhood Renewal: National Strategy Action Plan (Social Exclusion Unit, 2001) identified many problems that need to be addressed to overcome social exclusion. These include:

▶ being detached from society
▶ separation by a gulf of prosperity and opportunity
▶ poor educational attainment

- high crime rates
- high unemployment rates
- neighbourhoods locked into a spiral of decline.

Some solutions

The key question is 'can online learning make a significant contribution to addressing these needs and deficiencies?' There are several major initiatives underway which are directly or indirectly likely to support online learning. These include:

- Learndirect
- UK Online Centres
- Trade Union Learning Fund
- Learning and Skills Council
- National Neighbourhood Renewal Action Plan
- Basic Skills Strategy
- People's Network.

Key conclusion

- ICT is highly motivating and can attract people to return to learning. However, to fulfil its potential online learning must be able to make a substantial contribution to economic and social problems.
- To assist socially-disadvantaged people employ online learning requires staff with outreach, mentoring and tutoring experience and skills.
- There is a need for staff with community outreach, mentoring and tutoring skills to develop online and ICT skills.
- There is a need for staff with online learning skills to develop community outreach, mentoring and tutoring skills.

4 *Trends in technology and learning*

Considering the trends

One of the few certainties in information and communication technology (ICT) is that when you predict trends you almost always get them wrong. With this warning we will now attempt to consider the trends or factors that will influence ICT:

▶ There is an enormous interest in all sectors of the education and training world in developing online learning. Almost every educational institution, training provider and large organisation is considering the possibilities and many initiatives are underway.

▶ There are relatively few experienced online learning practitioners in Britain but many are being trained. However, it is uncertain if they will be sufficient (Salmon, 2000).

▶ A large proportion of online learning experience is currently based in higher education and large corporate users.

▶ A large proportion of the population does not see the relevance of ICT to their lives (IT for All, 1998). In contrast there is considerable interest in learning about ICT amongst adults who do see the relevance or who are willing to explore the possibility (Sargant, 2000).

▶ A large proportion (32%) of UK households have access to the internet (National Statistics, 2000) but many disadvantaged households do not.

▶ The power of the computer is continuously growing while its relative cost is falling.

▶ The availability of broadband (i.e. high-speed) access is growing but significant areas of the country and a large part of the population are unlikely to have access to a broadband connection in the next few years.

▶ The internet is expanding so that by 2010 it is estimated that 1 billion people will be using it.

▶ ICT has already had a major impact on the structure of organisations and continues to do so.

▶ High-quality computer-based learning materials are currently in short supply and skewed towards certain subjects such as ICT, management training and language learning (Clarke and Walmsley, 1999).

▶ Software tools are available in many forms to allow learners and tutors to create their own learning materials.

▶ People skilled in the design of online and computer-based learning materials are in short supply.

▶ Television and computing technologies are coming together so that access to the internet will become widely available through many different devices including television, games machines, telephone and mobile devices.

▶ Teleworking (both full- and part-time) is growing rapidly.

▶ Prolonged use of the internet appears to be linked to a reduction in social contact.

▶ Online learning is essentially neutral in that learners are invisible to each other and their tutors and can present themselves in any way they choose.

▶ Many professional tutors have little understanding of how to integrate ICT into their courses

This is the environment in which online learning is being established. It is one of contrasts, with vast enthusiasm but limited practical experience; of rapid growth in access whilst excluding some groups; of limited high quality learning materials but rapid expansion in provision; and of individual motivation to learn through online methods linked to a real risk of failure.

Key conclusion

▶ Predictions are unlikely to be completely accurate.

▶ The headline changes tend to disguise the real problems in employing online learning to overcome social exclusion.

5 *What is online learning?*

A wide range of approaches

Online learning is the outcome of a convergence of extant, new and emerging technologies with a range of education and training approaches. It is a broad term and includes computer-mediated learning, computer-mediated communication, web-based learning and instruction. It includes a whole range of options including individual and collaborative learning, informal and formal learning, downloadable learning materials, conferencing systems, student support, student/tutor interaction, student/student interaction and administration. The online aspect can relate to a single organisation's network or the whole internet.

Implementing online learning

Computer-based learning (CBL) has been used for in excess of 30 years and represents the coming together of the learning activity and computer technology. CBL offers the potential for learning to be delivered more flexibly, both in time and place. Large proportions of CBL materials were initially text-based, but gradually some degree of interactivity and inclusion of multimedia began to appear. As systems became technically more sophisticated there was accompanying growing concern about the efficiency and effectiveness of technology in the learning.

Commenting on comparative research in the computer-based training (CBT) field, Foshay (1994) points to the fact that such research has some value only if we recognise that differences in effectiveness and efficiency in delivering training are due primarily to the way in which CBT is designed and not to the mere fact that the training is on a computer. This is also true of online learning. There is no guarantee that simply putting a course online will lead to successful learning. The design of the course is one of the critical factors.

The general application of computing technology to education gave rise to much interest in the early 1980s. Computer-based education or computer-assisted learning developments were undertaken across a range of topics and subjects. There were expectations, for example, of a large growing industry for developing educational software and for artificial intelligence systems that would be able to encompass both the necessary domain knowledge with its structures and the delivery techniques normally resident in the teacher, tutor or trainer. Market expectations have not been met and artificial intelligence techniques have failed to develop the forecast capabilities. However, there is a well-established group of open learning suppliers in Britain (Clarke and Walmsley, 1999). They tend to specialise in particular sectors of the market or in supplying certain types of service (e.g. producing CBL). Suppliers of all types of open learning material tend to be small. The BASE survey of multimedia companies (1997) reported that 66 per cent of the companies who responded employed ten or less people and only 7.5 per cent employed more than 50.

The potential of online learning

Online learning has caught the imagination and interest of people working in education around the world (Owston, 1997). This is due to its potential to deliver, at relatively low cost, learning to the home, school, work and community. In its report, *Taking Training On Line*, for the Department for Education and Employment, the Epic Group (2000) offers a range of drivers for internet-based training – they define these as a subset of online learning. They are, in order of decreasing importance:

- making training more accessible
- reducing the time to deliver training
- seeing for yourself how valuable learning can be
- exploiting the organisation's internet and intranet facilities
- reducing the cost of training
- delivering a wider range of training content
- interest at senior management level
- demonstrating that the training department is keeping up
- demand from users.

A variety of writers have discussed what is essential about online learning. McManus (1995) highlights the importance of considering what is unique about the internet, while Khan (1999) proposes that an online learning environment should include resources and support which implements internet-based activities as part of a learning framework. Stefanov *et al.* (1998) suggests the need for a learning environment in which learners can meet, interact and work together as if they were face-to-face. Fuller *et al.* (2000) suggest that design of online environments needs to consider both the learning styles of the learner and the tutor's preferred teaching style.

The direction of many writers is to create an open and trusting environment by understanding the learner, encouraging the exploration of ideas and relationships and by helping them develop ownership of the learning. The challenge for the online environment in the development of autonomous life-long learners rests in its potential to help the learner:

- make decisions
- use new material
- make connections between and amongst items
- recognise and identify personal goals
- take personal responsibility for their learning.

The design or use of an online learning environment is very different from traditional education or training situations (e.g. the classroom).

Key conclusion

- Online learning is a general term covering a range of approaches.
- Simply transferring a course from a traditional setting to an online environment is no guarantee of success and is likely to fail. Learning materials and processes need to be adapted to the new situation.

6   *Online learning issues*

Different approaches

There are a number of approaches to supporting learning by the use of computer and communication technologies. The main approaches are:

- simple delivery of the learning materials to the learner (i.e. the learner downloads the package and either works interactively with it on their own computer or prints out the material to study away from the computer)
- lecture notes and visual aids being placed on the internet, intranet or network to aid students
- using the internet as a library of resources (e.g. electronic journals, online databases, reports and references)
- communication links between student and tutor (e.g. email, mailgroups, bulletin boards and electronic conferences)
- communication links between learners to provide mutual support (e.g. conferences, mailgroups and bulletin boards)
- communication links between tutors to provide mutual support (e.g. conferences and mailgroups)
- frequently asked questions websites
- interactive learning online (i.e. the learner works with a package at a remote location)
- computer learning environments
- computer-assisted assessment
- virtual seminars and conferences
- video and audio conferencing to provide face-to-face support for learners in remote locations or simply at a distance from a tutor.

Growing interest

The interest in all forms of online learning is huge and hundreds of different developments are underway in Britain. However, the proportion of learning delivered online is still relatively small. Within higher and further education the use of email to link the student and tutor is already well established but normally in the context of a conventional classroom or open learning course. It does not seem to be linked towards a move to a wider use of online methods. Equally the growth of conferencing and mail group facilities is significant so that many thousands of students have now the means to discuss issues with their peers and tutors. The Open University has provided conferencing and email services for several years and tens of thousands of students have taken part. Some of this communication is essentially enhancing informal learning that in a conventional sense would take place in corridors, canteens and through student/student interaction

More structured use of communication links is being developed so that email and conferencing are being integrated into course programmes. However, progress is slower than the explosive growth in the use of email. The Open University has begun to version existing modules to allow students to submit and receive feedback of assignments online. This involves tutors changing their approach to supporting learners (e.g. marking assignments on screen to provide faster feedback). This may seem a small step compared to many of the more exciting possibilities of new technology but does illustrate the practical difficulties of expanding online learning. The Open University already has thousands of students sending their assignments and receiving feedback by email. Within other institutions the scale is often smaller but many significant developments have been started. Many universities have developed or are developing courses based on the use of communication technology (e.g. Sheffield University, Manchester Metropolitan University, Oxford University and London University). International co-operation is already a part of online developments.

Methods such as virtual seminars and conferences are being used but are still relatively rare. The evidence suggests that they can be effective approaches, however they are significantly different from their conventional analogies. Online seminars often last many weeks or months and involve participants from many parts of the world. This removal of national borders for the delivery of learning is likely to be a major influence of online delivery of courses. At the moment only a small number of virtual seminars and conferences have been held and few evaluations have taken place. It is clear that practitioners are experimenting with the approaches and good practice is only just beginning to emerge.

Many further and higher education institutions are making learning materials available to students and others by placing them on internet and intranet sites. In the main these are paper-based workbooks or guides that you download and print. These are often linked to important generic topics such as IT skills, using the library and study skills. In some cases taster materials have been located on websites for prospective students to try out. In the USA several universities make course and learning materials available on their websites – the Massachusetts Institute of Technology has recently announced their intention to put all their materials online.

Using the internet

It is probable that most higher and further education institutions are implementing or considering how to use the internet to support their work. The large number of developments makes it difficult to analyse. The types of development frequently encountered are:

- paper-based learning materials available on a website for downloading
- internet-based assessment
- online seminars
- learning groups
- course information
- taster packs
- conferencing for courses

- mailgroups for courses
- access to library catalogues
- links to websites containing useful resources
- CVs of academic staff
- research papers
- Virtual Learning Environments (e.g. simulations, microworlds and virtual reality).

Commercial training material developers are beginning to use the internet to distribute their products, or offer some form of after sales support or market their materials. This seems to be mainly based on allowing prospective customers to view review copies of the materials and following purchase to download the material. In a parallel development large corporate users of multimedia and computer-based learning are carrying out a similar process based on their intranets.

Evaluation and research

Evaluation and research evidence to support different approaches is not readily available. There is little to help tutors or institutions compare approaches or identify effective practice. This is perhaps not surprising given the speed of development and the pace of change in this area. However, it is vital for exploitation of online methods to have access to the emerging evidence of good practice. For example distance learners have frequently been supported through telephone contacts – how will switching to email support affect their learning? The anecdotal evidence suggests a number of changes and that they are of mixed benefits to learners:

- more emails from students than telephone calls
- emails are less intrusive than telephone calls
- emails are shorter and more focused
- it is more difficult to diagnose problems by email
- the tutor can support more students by email
- email does not completely replace the need for occasional telephone calls or face-to-face meetings.

Key conclusions

- There is enormous interest in all forms of online learning across all sectors.
- Some online approaches (e.g. email communication) have already had a significant impact but work on many aspects is still at an early stage.
- Independent evidence of effective practice is slowly emerging.
- There is a major need for research evidence.

6.1 *Online learners*

A wide range of learners

The stereotypical description of successful open learners is that they are motivated, mature and confident people often who have had a history of educational achievement (Simpson, 2000; Learning and Skills Development Agency, 2001). However, in contrast to these conclusions the evidence from the Open Learning Credits pilot programmes (Crowley-Bainton, 1995) demonstrated the suitability of open learning approaches for a wide range of adults who have been long-term unemployed. In this case the materials and structure were designed to follow the best practice available. Materials were chosen to be high quality and regular contact with tutorial support was an important element in the programme. This perhaps indicates that students with limited learning skills and confidence can successfully use open and distance learning providing adequate support is made available.

The correct provision to develop the required skills

The evaluation of the Open Credits pilot programmes suggest that it would be useful to provide:

- initial study skills training
- face-to-face support either individually or in groups
- contact with other students
- proactive contact by tutors
- mentoring support.

Other successful attempts have been made to provide open learning for disadvantaged adults and communities. A Learning Methods Project (1993) was undertaken to provide training in four communities (Sunderland, Bradford, Lewisham and Wandsworth). This demonstrated that open learning was successful if good practice was followed. This included:

- providing information, advice and guidance
- offering tutorial support
- targeting and marketing opportunities
- managing the provision
- planning and monitoring the programme.

A number of writers and researchers have considered the characteristics of successful online learners. The California Distance Learning Project (1997) suggested four general characteristics of successful distance learners. These are:

- voluntary learning
- motivated, ambitious and self-disciplined learning
- a tendency to be older than the average student
- a tendency to posses a serious attitude to the course.

Supporting learners

Nipper (1989) suggested that successful online learners are active and creative people. Although this was the conclusion of an early use of online learning it is supported by anecdotal evidence that emphasises motivated, experimenting and participative learners. Several researchers have identified that the relationship between learners is important in all forms of learning. Peer support is important; it has been shown to be a useful addition in many forms of learning including information and communication technology (ICT) (Clarke, 1998). Nipper (1987) reported that learners needed to be able to relate and work together as part of the online learning process. This is very similar to the needs of a traditional group of learners.

Some online workers would probably suggest that this supportive relationship is more important in online learning than a traditional classroom. However, there is little objective evidence for this conclusion. Several writers have suggested that online groups need to have an initial face-to-face meeting in order to begin the process of forming a group and developing personal relationships with each other and their tutors. This is often a practice suggested in the open and distance learning literature. It is intended to reduce the effects of isolation by quickly establishing a relationship between participants. The transition from traditional approaches to online learning can be difficult for learners. A key part of the transition is to become competent and confident users of the technology. Palloff and Pratt (1999) reported that individual confidence with the technology was likely to enhance a feeling of well-being and increase the possibility of successful participation in online learning.

Online discussion

Email has the major advantage of being a quick straightforward method of communication. Although it is an asynchronous communication channel it is possible to have an electronic conversation due to the speed of the approach if learners are at both ends of the transfer. Learning is often undertaken through discussion. An email discussion is different from a face-to-face discussion in that each participant will join or leave the discussion at different times. Each learner will contribute at different times so there may be a less logical flow than in a face-to-face discussion. It easier to have an argument or to express offensive views using email so it is important that participants work within a code of behaviour. This is usually called 'netiquette'. It is often seen as good practice to allow the learners to agree the code of conduct. Understanding the nature of email discussion is a critical issue for online learners.

There is a variety of evidence that proposes that online learning may be beneficial to some learners. Palloff and Pratt (1999) reported that online learning would help some students who were not successful learners in traditional settings. They identified that it had the potential to assist quiet learners to be more active participants. In face-to-face discussions it is easier for forceful personalities to dominate the discussion, while online debates are completely open and it is impossible for anyone to prevent a contribution from another participant.

Learners dissatisfied with traditional methods

A great deal has been written about the potential of the computer to aid learners who have found traditional learning/teaching approaches unsatisfactory. This has been reported from the first introduction of the BBC and microcomputers with primary schools in the 1980s through to the use of the latest technology today. The reasons for the positive effects have been related to:

- the motivational effect of being given access to expensive, modern technology which the learner would not normally be able to use
- patience, in that computers will never become annoyed no matter how many attempts the learner has to make to achieve the desired outcome
- one-to-one support is available from the computer
- value-free – computers treat everyone the same and are free of stereotypes.

To successfully use online learning requires a range of skills that are discussed later in more detail. They are broadly a mixture of technical (how to use ICT equipment and software) and learning skills. In both cases the learner needs to be competent.

It is clear that in order to be successful an online learner requires a range of skills, knowledge and attitudes. These include motivation, confidence, technical skills, learning and creativity. For disadvantaged adults, who may have had few opportunities to learn, poor experience of education and training, and are returning to learning after an interval of many years, these characteristics are likely to be under developed. Online learning needs to provide support to develop the skills, knowledge and attitudes of a successful learner.

Key conclusion

- Successful online learners need a range of skills which people returning to learning are not likely to have fully developed. Online learning needs to provide the means of developing the required skills.
- Online learning in the community needs to be provided in the context of creating an infrastructure of support. This will require community development strategies to be undertaken in parallel with online learning and integrated with them.

6.2 Tutorial support

Online support

Both online and offline support are required for successful online learning. This section considers online support while the next focuses on offline. This distinction is simply for presentation, both are essential and are best provided in combination, integrated together.

Tutor competence is essential for online success

Tutors are an important part of all learning programmes and online learning is no exception. The Campaign for Learning (2000) survey of online learners reported that 11 per cent of their sample reported that it was not possible to learn without other people and that 96 per cent wanted personal support with their learning. Jung (2000) suggests that the tutor's skills as a facilitator are critical to the success of online learning. Anecdotal evidence stresses the positive relationship between good support and learner retention.

Tutors need to be both competent with information and communication technologies (ICT) and skilled in the use of technology to aid learning. At present the number of online tutors in Britain is small. There is a need to train large numbers of teachers to be competent in employing online and other computer-based techniques to aid learning (Learning and Skills Development Agency, 2001). Harasim *et al.* (1995) suggests that a tutor who is not able to facilitate online activities may produce a poor learning experience. Freenburg (1998) discusses the importance of online tutors realising that the appropriate use of the environment is vital to the learning experience. Competent online tutors are crucial to the success of online learning. The skills required by online tutors are likely to include:

- developing learners' online learning skills
- developing learners' confidence and motivation
- providing effective feedback through email, annotating electronic documents and conferencing (e.g. video, audio and text conferencing)
- facilitating collaborative and individual learning
- appropriate technical skills
- flexibility and adaptability
- designing online learning materials and programmes
- moderation of discussion in both small and large mailgroups
- supporting individual and group activities.

Whitlock (2000) suggests ten key tasks for online tutors. These are:

- diagnosing learners' needs
- helping learners' to get started
- explaining content
- assessing progress
- giving feedback
- promoting activity
- giving encouragement
- trouble-shooting problems
- preparing the learning environment
- recording progress.

Salmon (2000) provides a table of e-moderator online competencies with five characteristics. These are:

- understanding of the online process
- technical skills
- online communication skills
- content expertise
- personal characteristics.

Salmon feels that there are relatively few people with the necessary skills at the moment.

Online tutors' skills have several things in common with traditional face-to-face skills, especially those relating to facilitating groups and motivating individuals. The significant difference is that communication is through ICT rather than in person. This means that communication frequently involves a time lag between sending and receiving a message and relies heavily on short written messages. It is easy to emphasise these differences, but there are also differences between what is needed by skills tutors and for other traditional approaches (e.g. delivering a lecture compared to facilitating a workshop).

The need for staff development

Many tutors express doubts about their own technical skills and understanding of ICT. This often manifests itself as a lack of confidence in their ability to support learners who are using a computer-based approach. Although tutors express their doubt in terms of technology, the need is often associated with how to use ICT and learning in the context of their subject (e.g. how to use a word processor to help deliver basic skills).

Many online tutors are relatively inexperienced so they are essentially learning about these methods alongside their learner. This may make them adopt more conservative methods. It also means there is a need for online tutors to be able to share experiences and provide each other with mutual support. Several authors have also reported that an online tutor's workload is considerably higher than for a comparable conventional course (Tolley, 2000).

A simple conclusion is to state that there is a need for staff development on several levels. These include:

▶ ICT knowledge and skills – tutors must be competent and confident users of the technology
▶ online tutoring skills (e.g. developing online learning skills and exploiting communication technologies)
▶ supporting learners at a distance.

However, the practical issues of providing staff development to adult tutors with experience of socially- or economically-disadvantaged adults should not be under-estimated. Many tutors are part-time so that there are major logistical barriers to overcome. The availability of skilled and experienced trainers to provide the training is limited and even access to ICT is by no means universal.

Key conclusion

▶ Online tutors are essential in online learning.
▶ There is a need to provide staff development on a large scale.

6.3 Other forms of support

Offline support

Learner support does not have to be exclusively online and a combination of face-to-face and distance support needs to be available. Many learners will access online learning through learning centres and staff of the centres are a key part of the support network. The staff roles within learning centres obviously vary but to some extent everyone is involved in supportive activities. Their roles can be described in a variety of ways but all have similarities to coaching and mentoring. There is a considerable body of anecdotal evidence that learning centre staff play a vital role in supporting learners. However, the first step in supporting learners is to encourage them to visit the centre and help them begin to learn. This requires the application of outreach skills and approaches combined with an appropriate learning centre environment.

Good practice

The Further Education Funding Council Inspectorate (FEFC, 2000), reporting on practice in open and distance learning in further education colleges, identified a range of good practices including:

- provision of individual mentors
- initial assessment of learners' needs
- initial face-to-face briefing of learners including meeting their peers
- self-assessment of the suitability of possible courses of study
- self-assessment of learners' own abilities
- tutorial support available on a face-to-face or video conferencing basis
- good quality appropriate learning materials.

One of the main benefits of computer-based learning is widely reported as its ability to provide interactive, personalised and supportive learning experiences. This does not happen automatically, the material must be designed to achieve these results. Computer-based training has been designed with the intention of providing training that will need the minimum of human support. It is therefore perfectly possible to design online learning materials that will support the learner. The degree to which these products can provide all the required support will depend upon the learners' needs and experience.

This list of good practice provides a reasonable outline of the types of support that are needed for online learners. Simpson (2000) suggested that support is both academic and non-academic. Both types of support are needed and need to be integrated. Support is the responsibility of everyone involved with the learner and involves many different actions. It is related to the type of online learning being provided – online aspects may only be a small part of a course or the course may be entirely based on the use of technology.

Types of offline support

Some possible support approaches, actions and methods include providing:

- clear information about the course and what it requires from the learner
- initial advice and guidance to help learners identify if online learning is suitable for them
- initial briefing or induction for learners
- initial face-to-face meetings between learners and tutors
- assistance with developing and improving learning skills
- opportunities for self-assessment
- practical support within learning centres
- peer support
- learning materials designed to supply help and assistance.

This list demonstrates that support consists of many different activities. These need to be integrated together so that a support network is created to meet the learners' needs. It is unlikely that there is one perfect model of learner support since this will depend on the characteristics of the learners, nature of the course or learning opportunities, the environment and the educational culture (Tait, 2000).

Key conclusion

- Support should not be limited to a narrow range of strategies. Online learning should be seen as complimentary to other learning support activities.
- Support staff are essential to the success of online learning and a major staff -development programme is needed.

6.4 *Wider participation*

Technology overcoming physical barriers to partcipation

Computer-based and online learning offer considerable possibilities for opening up learning opportunities for adults who would otherwise have considerable difficulties in taking part. These include:

▶ screen readers for visually impaired learners – these read the display to the learner using synthesised speech thus allowing them access to online learning materials. Websites and other online learning materials need to be designed so that they will work with the screen reader and not against it

▶ a variety of software applications are available which help people with dyslexia to produce quality written documents

▶ standard applications (e.g. Microsoft Windows) sometimes include facilities to adjust them to be more suitable for disabled users (e.g. font size, contrast and using the keyboard as an alternative to the mouse)

▶ many types of input device which provide an alternative to the keyboard and standard mouse. These include speech input, switch interfaces, speech synthesis – output, key guards and roller balls

▶ communication technologies which allow learners to take part in online seminars, conferences and tutorials, and to discuss their studies with fellow learners who would otherwise be unable to travel to the physical location. For many disabled adults one of their most supportive environments is their own home with technology that, enabling them to participate from their homes, can potentially be extremely powerful

▶ tools that automatically translate the predominantly English content of the internet into other languages to widen participation

▶ access to online newspapers covering other parts of the world

▶ communicating with other learners in different parts of the world to share experiences and develop understanding

▶ simulations of situations, equipment or environments that would be very difficult to experience. Multimedia and virtual reality techniques can allow learners to explore and experiment with complete freedom.

Limiting factors

Although, there is a huge potential for positive gain from information and communication technologies (ICT) it is not a solution to all problems. There is a need for more research and development to turn potential into reality and also to ensure that new problems do not replace old ones. A more immediate issue is that the current solutions need to be known and understood by tutors. In a report to the Department of Trade and Industry about ICT and disabled users, Carey (1999) argues that a lack of awareness of the technical solutions is the key limitation to realising the current possibilities. Anecdotal evidence suggests that many tutors do not have a good understanding of the wide range of adaptations, alternative equipment and approaches available. This is perhaps not surprising with many tutors still developing their own ICT skills.

Another significant limitation to realising the potential of ICT is that designers of online materials and websites need to design products that allow access solutions, such as screen readers, to work. Neilson (2000) suggests that making a website accessible to visually impaired users requires little beyond using HTML to include meaning into the design and not simply appearance. Nevertheless, there are many examples of sites being largely inaccessible because of a lack of understanding.

The current situation is that ownership of computers and access to the internet is below the national average for disabled people (OFTEL, 2000; Russell and Drew, 2001; BECTA, 2001). This suggests the potential for widening participation amongst disabled people and those with learning difficulties has yet to be fully realised.

Key conclusion

▶ Technology can provide adaptations and aids to overcome many of the physical barriers to participation. However, understanding of them is limited amongst practitioners.

6.5 Collaborative learning

Isolated learning

Open and distance learning is frequently associated with individual or even isolated learning. The individual is working with a package of materials on his or her own in many cases at home. Contact with other students is often limited to an occasional tutorial, weekend residential or other meeting. These are frequently extra activities in that they are not compulsory and students can choose to take part or not. The students are very clearly individual learners. Learners' contact with their tutors is equally limited in traditional forms of open and distance learning. It is often no more than the comments on assignments, an occasional telephone call and a rare face-to-face meeting. This isolation is not necessarily negative in that many learners successfully complete their courses of study. However it does seem to put a great deal of emphasis on the students learning skills, they need to be able to:

▶ manage their time
▶ cope with a minimum of support
▶ be self-sufficient and confident learners.

This indicates that successful open and distance learners are likely to have well developed learning skills and possibly a record of success in education and training.

Linking learners and their tutors

Communication technologies have been used to provide additional support, as well as linking learners together and learners with their tutors. Many practitioners have recognised that early technologies such as the fax and telephone could be helpful to link people together. The advent of email, electronic conferencing and mailgroups provided a more powerful means of overcoming isolation and helping learners to mutually support each other. In open and distance learning courses these technologies were quickly introduced as an additional element. In many cases however, they were not integrated into the course. This was rapidly shown to be ineffective with a low rate of use and participation in electronic conferences and mailgroups. Course designers realised that to be successfully used online elements need to be integrated into the course activities. This is another example where simply providing extra resources does not lead inevitably to their effective use.

Collaborative or co-operative learning

These approaches are essentially extensions of traditional open and distance learning practice. They are still largely based on individual learners working alone but with the extra opportunities to meet other learners electronically and to have easier access to their tutors. These features are likely to be powerful aids to learners if used effectively. Another distinct approach, which is to some extent a departure from traditional open and distance learning practice, is collaborative or co-operative learning. This is where groups of learners work together using communication technologies to jointly carry out learning activities (McConnell, 2000). It is based on the established practice that there are learning benefits in small groups of learners working on a common task.

Communication technology allows groups to be formed from individuals who are physically separated.

It has been suggested that collaborative or co-operative learning has extensive benefits (Slavin, 1990; Sharan, 1990). Some of these may be particularly useful to adults returning to learning. They include:

▶ increased personal confidence and motivation
▶ opportunities to develop positive relationships with other learners
▶ opportunities to develop a positive attitude towards learning
▶ opportunities to develop a positive attitude to learning to learn.

Traditional versus online collaborative learning

Many practitioners have considered peer support as a key component in helping learners in both traditional classroom and open and distance learning situations. Collaborative or co-operative online learning is essentially based on this good practice. Table 1 compares traditional and online collaborative learning.

Table 1 Comparing traditional and online collaborative learning

Aspects	Traditional	Online	Discussion – online aspects
Communication	Verbal Written Visual	In most cases written text	Basic skills are critical to online learning since it assumes competency in written skills however it does provide access to spelling and grammar checkers
Time	Immediate since largely face-to-face or spread over a defined period	Normally asynchronous with activities spread over a period	Pressure is reduced due to the limited need to react immediately Learners need to manage their time Timescales are more flexible so learning can be undertaken when most convenient to the learner. It can be frustrating waiting for other learners to respond Learners can carefully consider their contribution

Aspects	Traditional	Online	Discussion – online aspects
Equality	People are free to form their own judgements of each other	Individuals can present themselves as they wish so judgements are potentially free of prejudice	Learners are potentially able to achieve equal treatment from other group members. However, this is relatively untested or investigated
Contributions	Face-to-face groups tend to be based on one individual addressing the rest of the group	Messages can be sent at any time so communications are multi-way and complex	There is equal opportunity to contribute and groups are not as easily dominated by particular individuals

Table 1 suggests that there are distinct benefits to be achieved from online collaborative approaches compared to traditional group methods. However in practice there are also some negative aspects, these include:

▶ group members are free to take part or not so it can be frustrating if some members of the group are not willing to join in when others want to move forward. This is also true of traditional collaborative groups but perhaps more easily overcome, individuals can avoid taking part more easily in online groups
▶ online messages are often short, to the point and can be unintentionally offensive which can lead to fierce online arguments
▶ contributions from individuals and tutors are more limited and less subtle so that it is difficult to vary your role (e.g. peace-maker, devil's advocate, etc.).

Most tutors who employ group-learning methods are aware that they must support the groups and achieve this by regularly sitting in during the discussions to check that everyone is being included and that there are no problems. Tutors need to find a balance between sitting in and probably influencing the discussion by their presence, and allowing groups to become bogged down and unable to progress. Online groups are easier to monitor in that the tutor can read all the communications and can therefore precisely judge their interventions. However, since they cannot see each learner they have no means of knowing if silence indicates thoughtful reflection of the issues, confusion or simple non-interest. The only means that they have is to send the individual a message to check what is happening.

Using collaborative learning

Online collaborative learning has been used for a wide range of activities. The list below is only for illustrative purposes since new areas are continuously being developed. Activities include:

- business studies
- teaching skills
- open learning
- information and communication technologies
- women's studies
- professional development.

Key conclusion

- Collaborative learning has major benefits in online learning, similar to those in more traditional approaches. However, there are also significant differences in practice.
- Online collaborative learning presents significant staff development challenges.

6.6 *Vicarious learning*

Lurking

A widely reported phenomenon is 'lurking'. This is when only a minority of learners take part in an online forum of some type (e.g. mailgroups, online seminars and conferences). Frequently a minority of participants take part by sending contributions while the lurkers are able to read the messages and experience the dialogue but do not contribute. This is regarded as beneficial by the learners who lurk (Petre *et al.*, 2000). This process has also been called vicarious learning.

This process is probably similar to sitting at the back of a class and listening to the discussion while not contributing to the debate. In a physical classroom a teacher or tutor would attempt to encourage participation to ensure that everyone had the opportunity to contribute. This is mainly to ensure that the more confident extrovert learners do not dominate the discussion. However, in the online situation it is not possible to dominate the debate. The technology provides everyone with an equal opportunity to take part but a majority rarely offer their views. This limits the potential richness of the communication.

Encouraging participation

In a traditional class a learner who does not contribute to the discussion during the first meeting or two often finds it increasingly difficult to make a contribution. It is a key tutor task to help learners to take part early to prevent this barrier. In an online group there is probably a similar requirement for the tutor/facilitator to assist the learner to make an early contribution. Another factor may also need to be considered. In face-to-face groups the fluency and volume of contribution of some learners effectively silences other people, in online situations some people do send far more messages than others. Is this another factor preventing contributions?

It is difficult to explain why many learners choose not to send messages. It may be linked to the permanent nature of a written message compared to a verbal comment. Lurking has been reported in many groups but there may be a relationship with the size of group. In a traditional setting few people would make a contribution in a lecture theatre with several hundred other people but they might in a small group. Mailgroups are often communities of hundreds of people who, although invisible, may still deter the less confident participants. An approach that has been used in a variety of online courses has been to include contributions to the groups as part of the assessment so that there is a strong motivation to taking part. However, this does seem to penalise the quiet learner and those who have nothing to say. Other methods include group working as part of the course methods so that learners have to work with others to achieve an outcome.

These types of approaches do detract from the key benefits of online learning, to providing the learner with more choice in the place, pace and timing of their learning experience; they reduce the freedom of learners. Learners who have returned to learning after a long interval may have limited confidence so this may be a key factor in discouraging them from contributing. They will therefore be at a disadvantage if contributions are assessed as part of the course. It is perhaps better practice to encourage learners to make a contribution. Tutors are able to communicate privately with any learner so that they are able offer assistance and encouragement without everyone else being aware. This type of proactive tutoring is likely to achieve results and is probably more appropriate for learners who lack confidence or experience of online learning. The move from traditional approaches to online learning can be a struggle for some learners. However, it does appear to help some learners to express themselves and motivate them to become successful learners (Palloff and Pratt, 1999). Nipper (1989) feels that learners need to be confident and secure in the groups before they will be willing to contribute. This will need time to achieve and is a key role for the online tutor/facilitator.

Key conclusion

▶ Online learning will present new problems and challenges in securing active and effective learners.

6.7   *Design of materials*

Initiatives to develop open learning

There is a considerable tradition of designing open and distance learning materials in Britain. During the last 20 years there have been several national initiatives to stimulate the use and design of open learning such as the Open Tech programme. The Manpower Service Commission's Learning Technology Unit provided development funds for a wide range of computer-based learning projects to stimulate the development of innovative and effective learning products to meet identified learning needs. These initiatives have made a contribution to develop a core of people and organisations that have the skills and understanding to design open and distance learning materials.

These initiatives have also assisted the development of a network of organisations throughout the country that are able to support open and computer-based learning development. However, this is a relatively limited infrastructure, many of the commercial organisations are small- and medium-sized enterprises while education and training organisations often only have small teams or individuals operating in this area. The current enormous interest and growth in all forms of open learning, particularly online, has shown the need for substantial growth in the availability of designers and organisations able to develop learning materials.

Shortage of qualified tutors

This limited availability of expertise is perhaps best illustrated by the lack of quality learning materials. It is fairly easy to find people who have had a poor experience with some form of open learning material. This is not just due to poor design but is complicated by assumptions made during development. A product designed as an integrated element in a taught course is probably not suitable for use as a standalone system. It is likely to be criticised and misunderstood. This perhaps indicates that there is a shortage of tutors who have a detailed understanding of how to use open/computer-based learning.

Arenicola Design (2000) investigated the skills required to design computer-based learning materials and concluded that existing designers were relatively inexperienced and their training was not comprehensive with areas such as instructional design often being neglected. Jung (2000) concluding on the experience of the Korean National Open University stated that instructional design was critical for quality learning materials. The Campaign for Learning survey of adult learners (2000) reported that 26 per cent of learners perceived materials as poor, 20 per cent felt they were too 'gimmicky' and 20 per cent had difficulties accessing them.

Designing effective materials and courses

Designing effective online learning materials and courses is difficult due to a number of factors, although the physical process of producing materials is relatively straightforward. There are a wide variety of software tools to help the developer, also encouraging the enthusiast to develop materials. Nevertheless the tools do not provide them with the understanding of instructional design, learning, interaction, assessment and the other processes required to produce high quality learning materials. The danger is that they will try to reproduce a conventional learning environment or structure rather than exploit the different opportunities provided by computer-based learning (Freenberg, 1998).

Reeves and Reeves (1997) have proposed a model of internet-based interactive learning. This has ten dimensions that are each in turn a continuum of choices:

- pedagogical philosophy
- learning theory
- goal orientation
- task orientation
- source of motivation
- teacher role
- metacognitive support
- collaborative learning
- cultural sensitivity
- structural flexibility.

The authors do not claim this is a complete list of the dimensions but it does illustrate the complexity of the issues. The list does not include the integration of the different media (e.g. text, graphics, animation, sound and video) into the material, that itself is a highly skilled task. A designer must produce learning materials that allow for all possible learners responses, are supportive, motivating, technically stable (i.e. they will not fail) and have a suitable content. This is not straightforward, it requires considerable skills. Commercial developers employ a team approach combining:

- project management
- instructional/learning design
- graphical design
- technical skills
- subject expertise
- evaluation.

Current material and courses

Hara and Kling (2000) reported that students had three types of frustrations with online courses. These were a lack of prompt feedback, ambiguous instructions on the internet and technical problems.

Adults returning to learning after a considerable break and who may have had poor experience of formal education are likely to need material that is highly supportive since their learning skills will often be underdeveloped. Little material of this type has been created, in any format. Computer-based learning materials have largely been concentrated on schools and large organisations. The subjects covered by computer-based learning materials for adults are largely concentrated on commercial topics such as management training, information technology and language learning (Clarke and Walmsley, 1999). There is now more interest in producing supportive material but little material is yet available for areas such as basic skills. It will take a considerable investment over many years to produce an adequate national resource. When considering social exclusion, technology and the learning society, IBM (1996) concluded that technology had the potential to provide particular benefits for excluded groups. However, they identified a 'lack of appropriate training materials and delivery mechanisms'. The Policy Action teams report into the digital divide (DTI, 2000) identified that content is often unattractive or unsuitable for people in socially-deprived communities. Clarke and Walmsley (1999) reported that there was very little material in minority languages while the Fabian Society (2001) state that there is a lack of online content suitable for excluded people. This all contributes to the conclusion that, there are few specifically designed online learning opportunities for adults entering into learning and this is likely to reduce its potential for overcoming the barriers that disadvantaged learners face. The danger is that many learners will begin courses, but fail to complete them.

Key conclusion

- Design of online learning is key to the success of the approach.
- Online learning materials are not widely available and significant gaps exist in provision.
- Design skills are in short supply.

6.8 *Learning to learn*

The importance of online learning skills

Using information and communication technologies (ICT) to deliver and support learning requires learners to have appropriate learning skills. In many cases we are assuming that learners are studying on their own with their peers only available through communication links. To make effective use of communication technologies requires at least good written communication skills, search skills to locate material on the internet and learning styles which suit content/resource materials. It is probable that a proportion of the population will have limited learning skills or styles, which will make ICT-supported approaches unsuitable.

The learning skills required for successful online learning include:

- reflection
- time management
- acceptance of responsibility
- self-assessment
- analysis
- working in a collaborative team
- searching for information
- transferring learning to other situations
- communication skills (e.g. written)
- revision.

Collis and Meeuwsen (1999) suggest five areas for learning skills to be developed which are appropriate to online learners. These are:

- articulation and reflection
- planning
- study skills
- finding and applying relevant examples
- self-evaluation.

The two lists broadly agree and overlap.

The power of the internet as a source of information is not in doubt. Doring (1999) reminds us that in order to maximise its usefulness, users must become skilled at locating, selecting and assessing information. This is not a trivial task.

Adults returning to learning after a long break (possibly decades) and perhaps with a previously poor experience of education are unlikely to have good general and up-to-date learning skills. At the moment most adults will have little experience of online learning methods and only a minority of open learning. This suggests that there is a considerable need for online learning skills to be developed by almost all learners.

Developing online learning skills

The development of learning skills almost always takes place within another learning programme. This seems the most appropriate way, as learners are motivated to take part in the course, whereas a special course on learning skills may seem an additional barrier to the desired objective. However, in many cases the design of the learning programme has not considered the need to improve learning skills. Many adults are faced with learning by trial and error. For adults returning to learning who may lack confidence, this approach is likely to add to their difficulties. The learning programme needs to be designed to provide a framework that will support the development of skills. This could involve methods such as:

- assignments which require learners to collaborate with their peers
- demonstrating how their learning can be transferred to other situations
- encouraging learners to reflect on their experiences
- including self-assessment processes
- establishing feedback systems which cover learning skills as well as the course content.

The Further Education Funding Council Inspectorate (FEFC, 2000), reporting on current practice in open and distance learning, stated that 'in many instances, however, colleges place insufficient emphasis on the study skills required'.

Key conclusion

- For learners to have a successful online experience it is essential that they have well developed learning skills.
- Online courses must contain opportunities to develop learning skills.

6.9 Characteristics of different approaches

Different approaches

There are a number of different communication technologies, however they all take two forms:

▶ asynchronous
▶ synchronous.

Asynchronous

Asynchronous technologies are methods that do not rely on the people being at either end of the communication channel. They include:

▶ email (one-to-one or one-to-many)
▶ bulletin boards (one-to-many)
▶ mailgroups (one-to-many)
▶ intranet and internet websites (one-to-many or many-to-many)
▶ online conferences and seminars (one-to-one, one-to-many and many-to-many).

These approaches are widely used and would seem natural to improve communications.

Synchronous

Synchronous technologies are methods that do rely on the people being at either end of the communication channel. A telephone is a synchronous approach but leaving a message on an answer machine is asynchronous. These approaches include:

▶ chat (a largely informal way of communicating of one-to-one and one-to-many and many-to-many)
▶ video conferencing (one-to-one and one-to-many))
▶ audio conferencing (one-to-one and one-to-many)
▶ collaborative working using groupware (groups of two or more people).

The different characteristics of communication technologies

Mailgroups

The nature of online communication is different from conventional approaches (e.g. classroom, syndicate groups, etc.). If we consider some of the permutations and alternatives of a mailgroup:

- people do not always read their mail immediately. The patterns of response to a message are therefore complex. Discussions can seem to be over and then suddenly come to life days or weeks after the original message
- people will often reply directly to the sender so that in the mailgroup it may seem that nothing is happening while a healthy debate is taking place out of sight. In some mailgroups direct mail is the majority of communications
- many members of mailgroups only send an occasional message. There appears to be some connection between subject focus of a mailgroup and the degree of participation (Nonnecke and Preece, 2000).

Online material

How users interact with online material is again not obvious. Attention spans tend to be short with browsing being the best way to describe the behaviour. There is some evidence that learners who tend to browse are the most knowledgeable and probably confident (Clarke, 1996). Many users will print webpages they want to read rather than study them on the screen so that it is important to design materials for both reading on the screen and as a document. The Campaign for Learning (2000) survey of online learners reported that 51 per cent of e-learners preferred to read information on the screen while 42 per cent preferred to print it. Younger learners preferred to read the screen while older learners preferred to print. Visually impaired learners can access the material using a screen reader (this reads the screen to the learner), however, it assumes the design of the material has considered this possibility.

The potential of different approaches

The potential of all these communication approaches has been tested at least on a limited scale. The pattern of use is complex in that many initiatives have experimented with different approaches. Some examples are:

- email – widely used to enhance communication between peers and tutors
- mailgroups – discussion groups/workgroups
- chat – almost as a virtual students union for informal conversation
- video conferencing – language learning, developing ICT skills, tutorials, assessment etc.

Almost any combination of this technology can be used to support learning, but simply providing the technology is unlikely to achieve the best results. The degree of success relies upon the tutors and support staff explaining the approach. A key frustration is technical problems and any online learning approach must aim to minimise difficulties and provide technical help. This can be a major challenge in that learners will need the system 7 days a week, 24 hours a day – help needs to be available at all times.

Table 2 illustrates the roles that different technologies might play in achieving different learning objectives.

Table 2 Comparing learning organisation objectives and communication technologies[1]

Learning organisation objectives	Communication technologies	Comment
Group formation	Email	Aids communication between members of the group
	Groupware	Collaborative working
	On-line conferences and seminars	Aids cross-group learning
Cross-group learning	Email	Aids cross-group communication
	Mailgroup	Large scale discussions
	Intranet	Equal access to information
Developing a learning culture	Email	Aids cross-team communication
	Bulletin board	Share ideas
	Chat	Access to informal communication
Learning from experience	Mailgroup	Cross-organisation communication
	Online conferences and seminars	Aid to cross-organisational learning
Responsibility and authority is delegated	Internet and intranet sites	Easy, equal access to information
	Bulletin boards	Sharing information and ideas

Table 2 shows that different communication technologies have different benefits so it is important to select the most appropriate approach related to the learning objective.

Key conclusion

▶ Communication technology applications have different characteristics so their use has to be selective.

1 (based on Clarke, 2000)

6.10 *Moderating and facilitating*

Mailgroups

Mailgroups allow groups of learners to discuss issues in a way similar to face-to-face groups, but they are not limited to particular group sizes, or particular times. Mailgroups can be very large with hundreds of participants or small with only a few members. They are not limited by time so can run alongside an entire course of study or indeed independently of a particular course. A wide variety of benefits have been perceived in the use of mailgroups. Rojo and Ragsdale (1997) reported the following:

- keeping updated
- getting materials
- getting answers
- learning about the medium
- a feeling of belonging
- self-expression
- enhancing contacts.

Mailgroups are used for many different purposes including:

- sending a message to a large group of people (e.g. keeping learners informed efficiently and effectively)
- obtaining help and support by asking a group of people with similar interests a question through the mailgroup (i.e. peer support)
- discussing issues of common interest
- undertaking a group exercise as part of an online learning course
- providing resources to all learners.

The initial use of mailgroups was mainly to support groups of researchers and scholars who were separated by distance but shared areas of interest. Initially they were specialist discussion fora but have now developed to cover a vast range of topics and groups.

Mailgroups provide both a visible and invisible means of discussion. Participants are aware of emails sent to the group but since each email reveals the address of the sender it is perfectly possible to respond directly to the sender. Anecdotal evidence suggests that a great deal of all mailgroup traffic is invisible, it is directly to the sender rather than to the group. There is also another phenomenon known as 'lurking' where the user simply reads the messages and never or rarely sends a contribution. It is difficult to estimate the volume of useful lurking but estimates suggest that for each contributor there are three times as many readers or lurkers. This suggests that like an iceberg a lot is hidden beneath the surface in both lurking and direct emails. A straightforward analysis of the Making-IT-

Accessible mailgroup shows that on average three answers are provided for each question asked. This demonstrates the supportive nature of mailgroups.

Role of moderator

An important role in online learning communication is the moderator. This role does not have a direct equivalent in face-to-face learning support but it is similar to facilitating a group. Moderation is often associated with a mailgroup. The moderator attempts to encourage discussion by sending pertinent messages to the group. A successful moderator requires a wealth of good judgement to balance their interventions against interfering with mailgroup participants' own dialogue.

Moderators need to make their contributions without interrupting the discussion between participants so it is frequently suggested that they do not send too many messages but make a limited number of finely judged interventions. This is similar to intervening in a face-to-face group to help the flow of discussion or to encourage the debate to move in a particular direction. In an electronic discussion group the moderator has the additional option of sending email messages to a single participant. This is the equivalent of asking an individual in a face-to-face discussion to come for a chat in the corridor but without disrupting the other group members.

The direct email message can be used to suggest that an individual make a particular contribution, or equally to ask them to stop or to change their behaviour. This allows the moderator to assist the discussion while remaining in the background. Nevertheless there is a fine distinction between facilitating a learner-centred discussion and disguising a tutor-centred approach.

In addition to encouraging discussion moderation also involves:

▶ sorting out problems with joining and leaving the group
▶ providing information to prospective members
▶ welcoming new members
▶ answering questions
▶ providing information
▶ protecting members from offensive messages and essentially policing the group.

Styles of moderation may vary but a great deal of the communication is by direct email contact so it is hidden from the main group. It should not be forgotten that the moderator is also an individual member of the group so he or she also has a role simply as a participant.

Ways of contributing

It is important at the start of a mailgroup to agree some general rules to ensure that individuals are not offended or the group abused. Over time these are developed and enhanced and the group moderator needs to play a part in arbitrating when members ask for changes. Typical areas to consider include:

> ◗ offensive language
> ◗ messages should not make personal attacks on other members
> ◗ announcements – often members want to inform the group about events, publications or services which they have found useful
> ◗ attachments – large attachments often take a long time to download so groups often discourage members from including attachments
> ◗ viruses – attachments can be a source of virus infections so members need to ensure they do not send infected files and need to protect against them.

Individual contributions can take many forms including:

> ◗ individual questions
> ◗ answers and suggestions to resolve problems
> ◗ comments on issues which range from a single sentence to detailed responses covering several pages
> ◗ information, sources of resources or personal experience of learning aid products.

The order of discussion is frequently complex since each participant is free to read and respond to messages when it is convenient. Messages can arrive in strange sequences. There can be long gaps in discussions and responses can move in several directions simultaneously. This can be confusing but most people find it a refreshing approach and have few problems following the discussion. Messages that remain unread for even a short interval however can form an intimidating volume of email. Anecdotal evidence suggests that some individuals will simply delete all the mailgroup's messages and start again.

Mailgroups are very useful aids to online learning but require careful moderation to succeed. For the new or returning learners they are easy to contribute to since participants are essentially invisible and can present themselves in any way they choose. It is impossible for one individual to dominate the discussion and prevent other people from contributing, although some individuals contribute far more than others.

However, as mailgroups require contributions in writing, new learners or those with limited confidence or limited writing skills may find this restrictive. Also many mailgroups circulate archives of the discussion so people may be reluctant to make a spontaneous contribution that they otherwise would in face-to-face debate because it is a permanent record of their views.

Moderating or facilitating a mailgroup is still a new skill and most people involved would agree that they are in the process of learning how to undertake the task effectively. There is a need to share experience and good practice because the current information available is largely based on the experience of mailgroups and moderation in higher education.

Key conclusion

> ◗ Online approaches require new skills and practice to be developed. The dissemination of experience is vital to support the expansion of online learning.

6.11 *Location of access*

Location of online learning

One of the merits often given for online learning is that it can provide access to learning at many different locations including the:

▶ home
▶ learning centre
▶ work place.

Home

How does location influence learning? This is a critical question for the future of online learning and its success in delivering learning at the learner's choice of location. The image presented of the home learner is one of an individual who is able to simply switch on their computer or other device and take part in the learning. This seems a fulfilling and enjoyable experience but is this image correct?

Individuals studying at home are learning on their own in physical isolation from their peers. Most adult tutors would probably claim that a large element in a learning course is the opportunities it provides for adults to leave their homes, enjoy the social interaction with their peers and to establish new relationships. Online learning provides opportunities for communication and interaction but in different ways to a traditional course.

At the moment learners accessing online learning from home probably do so through a conventional telephone line with limited bandwidth so unless the design of the material takes this limited access into account it is likely to be slow. Equally important for adults is the phone bill, which, if they are online regularly is likely to be substantial. Again, the course designer can reduce these costs through the structure of the course.

Learning from home also means that learners are remote from technical support so if they encounter a problem it may well result in them being unable to take part in the course. It is possible to establish telephone helplines to provide technical assistance. Telephone helplines work best if learners have two telephone links so that the expert can talk them through the solution while they actually carry it out. This is not possible if you have only a single connection but mobile phones may satisfy this need. Telephone helplines almost always assume the individual's willingness to carry out technical tasks such as opening up the computer. This assumes a level of confidence many learners will not have. Technical problems can damage a learner's confidence and motivation so that a few poor experiences can result in them dropping out of the course.

So far we have considered online access through a personal computer, but it is already possible to use other systems including:

▶ digital television/internet ready sets
▶ hand-held devices
▶ games machines.

Television is largely a family or group experience so it is difficult to imagine how the family television could be used for studying. However, it would be possible to use the internet rather like an enhanced teletext service. Whilst hand held devices are excellent for messaging they are unlikely to be suitable for accessing large amounts of content due to the tiny screens they employ. Games consoles do offer the potential for online learning access, though currently there is no evidence that people are using them on a large scale for this purpose. Only a small percentage of homes exclusively use technologies other than the personal computer for internet access. Ninety-eight per cent access the internet through a personal computer (National Statistics, 2000).

Learning centre

Learning centres are being established in many different locations across the country – in libraries, colleges and many community sites. The learning centre is able to offer some key benefits to the user in that it is able to provide access to information and communication technologies (ICT), a good bandwidth, tutorial and technical support and peer interaction from a single venue. However, the critical factor is whether the centre is acceptable to socially- or economically-disadvantaged adults. Does it provide a friendly image to them or does it just seem like another institutional location that they are unwilling to enter? The organisation, image and structure of learning centres vary so it is difficult to give a general answer. Some other possible barriers are:

▶ the need to book appointments
▶ physical access for disabled or older learners
▶ limited access time
▶ the cost of courses and access to the internet (this varies considerably from nothing to several pounds an hour)
▶ the absence of a crèche or other forms of childcare.

There are many examples of successful community learning centres so it is possible to establish effective access to online learning through them. The Fabian Society (2001) emphasises the importance of centres being able to offer suitable social functions, such as a crèche or lunch club, to encourage participation. Learning centres need to be part of these wider activities in order to encourage participation. Outreach activities should be encouraged to integrate with the development of the centre.

It is important to realise that the use and familiarity with online resources is unlikely to be the same using a public computer as using one at home. In private learners are likely to explore, investigate and learn by doing more than in a public location, unless they are confident and secure in that environment.

For many adults, simply entering a learning centre is a major concern. Many centres have realised this and use outreach methods to build relationships and confidence before encouraging people to visit the centre.

Workplace

The workplace is often seen as an excellent location for online learning since the learners can use the computer on their desk to access the online resources when they are not busy. However, is the workplace a good location for online learning? Many offices can be stressful with background noise, continuous interruptions and a highly distracting environment. This is not ideal for concentrating on learning. The workplace is only going to be suitable if the social, organisational and physical environments are correct.

Some of the key factors for creating a successful learning environment are:

▶ peer support
▶ learning culture
▶ managerial support
▶ time to study in working hours – in particular make sure that learning is given at least equal status as the job so that learners are not continuously interrupted
▶ technical support
▶ mentoring/coaching.

Most of the discussion of workplace online learning tends to assume people have easy access to ICT. However, many workers do not have a computer or a desk. Are shop floor workers going to be excluded from these opportunities? How do they gain access to online facilities? It requires the organisation to develop an approach that gives them planned access to a learning centre or other resources when it is convenient for the workers. This has been undertaken in some companies. At the moment shop floor workers have as little access to online learning as to conventional training opportunities. Nevertheless it has been shown that for many people the workplace is an important location for learning (Sargant, 2000; DfEE, 1999).

An evaluation of delivering distance, flexible and online learning to small- and medium-sized enterprises has indicated that many small companies, although interested and motivated to use online learning, were not ready to create the necessary environment to ensure its success (Clarke, 2001). It was likely that they would need help in the form of outreach and other support to successfully implement online learning.

Key conclusion

▶ Although online learning provides the opportunity to use many different locations, in order to be successful sites require a supportive environment. Many potential locations are not ready to support online learning.

6.12 Costs and benefits

Cost is a critical factor

The critical factor in producing any form of computer-based learning material is the high initial cost. The Campaign for Learning (2000) survey of online learners reported that 49 per cent of providers felt that the costs of initiating and developing online learning were prohibitive.

The cost of production is often expressed in the form of a comparison with the cost of producing 1 hour of conventional learning material. To produce 1 hour of computer-based learning material requires between 20 and 100 times the effort than 1 hour of traditional material (Hunt and Clarke, 1997). The range is due to the different nature of the material (i.e. simple packages compared to those combining multimedia). This is a fairly crude method, however it does illustrate the major cost of producing computer-based learning of all types. It is possible to reduce the cost of online learning by reducing the reliance upon materials and placing the emphasis on mediated communication. This then results in the need for many skilled moderators/tutors.

Computer-based learning material is cost-effective mainly because it allows learning to be provided to large numbers of people. The unit cost is therefore reduced but this does require large-scale or long-term use of the material. Online learning provides the means of allowing large-scale access to computer-based learning so that it has the potential to use these materials in a highly cost-effective way, probably far in excess of other open learning approaches. However some authors have suggested that online learning requires more frequent updating than conventional open learning materials and also that workloads on tutors are higher (Weller, 2000).

Learning materials need to be integrated

In large organisations computer-based training has been employed for 2 decades largely as a standalone resource. Many organisations have developed materials that they believe requires very little or no support. This is probably accurate since they were often working with skilled, successful and highly motivated learners. The design of the material is intended to provide all the support that the learner requires. In schools educational software is often used in a distinctly different way to computer-based training in large organisations. Education software tends to be used in partnership with conventional methods so they are integrated together. Teachers are heavily involved with the learners.

Online learning has aspects of both these approaches and could adopt either or both. It allows many combinations of materials and tutorial support. Socially- or economically-disadvantaged adults are likely to need assistance even with material specifically designed to be supportive. This is probably going to increase the unit cost of online learning material, but if it is provided on a large enough scale then this is unlikely to be significant. More critical are the suitability of the design and the availability of trained moderators/tutors to support learners. There is still a great deal of work to be done to fully understand the factors that ensure cost effectiveness. Online learning is a new development and costs are not certain (Ng, 2000).

Key conclusion

▶ Materials have high initial development costs but online learning has the potential to minimise unit costs if used on a wide scale.
▶ Learning materials need to be integrated with support in a variety of forms in order to be effective.

6.13 *Retention*

Reasons for dropping out

All open and distance learning approaches tend to suffer from high drop out rates. This is often related to factors such as:

- a lack of learning support
- the isolation of learning at a distance from both other learners and tutors
- the stress of learning in a new way which is compounded if the learner is returning to education and training after a substantial break
- problems (e.g. work, family or other issues)
- a lack of confidence which is especially apparent in people returning to learning
- a fear of failing which is often associated with poor previous experience of education
- under-developed learning skills (e.g. note taking, analysis and time management). Again this is more apparent in those returning to learning
- an inappropriate selection or course design.

These factors are apparent in all forms of open learning. However, in online learning extra factors are also evident, including:

- stress when using information and communication technologies (ICT) equipment if you are new to the technology
- stress when using inappropriately designed ICT learning systems.

The Open University's experience indicates that a lack of educational success is the best predictor of dropping-out of an open and distance learning course (Simpson, 2000). Fifty per cent of learners with no previous educational qualifications drop out of open and distance courses while only 20 per cent of learners with a previous degree level qualification drop out.

It is difficult to measure retention rates since it depends on determining whether learners are still active (FEFC, 2000). Many open and distance learners will take longer to complete a course than traditional learners and will have dormant periods so that it is difficult to tell whether they are still part of the course or have dropped out. Achievement rates in further education colleges for open and distance learning are lower than other methods of learning (FEFC, 2000) probably due to a substantial number of dropouts. This illustrates a major issue for online learning and adults returning to learning. For many disadvantaged adults enrolling is a significant step. If they are then unable to continue they may never make the attempt to learn again.

Overcoming the barriers

To realise the potential of online learning to overcome the barriers faced by disadvantaged adults requires that the structure of the courses must aim to retain learners. Some features of an effective environment are:

- support from both pro-active and reactive peers, tutors and everyone else involved – providing assistance is a crucial role for all online staff
- learning materials especially designed for returning learners
- flexibility to allow learners to integrate learning into their lives
- guidance in selecting the course
- technical help and a reliable product.

Compaq Computer Ltd (MORI, 1999) investigated the incidence of computer rage. The study was based on a view that as computers become more complex the potential for user frustration and anger grows. All computer and software suppliers are attempting to provide products that are easy to use and easy to understand. However it is clear that it is not easy to provide products that meet these objectives.

The investigation focused on employees who use ICT. These are people who are largely competent computer users. It identified that computer rage was often associated with a lack of understanding of the technology. The rage took the form of verbal abuse of the computer, refusal to allow applications to be upgraded since this might lead to problems, refusing to use the computer or limiting their use and wasting time trying to solve computer problems (being distracted from the real work).

For new computer users the danger is that they will suffer even higher degrees of stress. This, combined with the other factors that cause learners to drop out, suggests that the risk for returning learners using online methods is likely to be significant.

Preparing learners

There is clearly a danger that socially-disadvantaged adults will be encouraged to take part in online learning only to be faced with many different pressures and stresses that significantly reduce the likelihood of success. There is a need to prepare returning learners for the challenge of online learning. This preparation will need to include:

- developing learning skills appropriate to the online environment
- developing ICT skills
- developing confidence
- coping with stress.

In addition the online environment will have to provide adequate support to ensure that isolation and distance is not overwhelming. Retention is a real problem that needs to be investigated so that approaches to minimise dropouts can be adopted.

7 *Social issues*

It is widely suggested that online learning has the potential to overcome social exclusion due to its ability to be delivered at a place, pace and time to meet individual needs. However, this is a simplistic statement in that people who are socially- and economically-disadvantaged often have a range of barriers to overcome and these vary between individuals. This section takes this simple analysis further to consider issues such as the nature of disadvantaged communities, access to the internet and many other factors which relate to realising the potential of online learning.

7.1 *Socially-excluded communities*

Disadvantaged communities and the delivery of online learning

This section will describe and consider the characteristics of socially- and economically-disadvantaged communities and the implications for the effective delivery of online learning. Drawing on a range of sources (Clarke, 1999; Maynard, 1998; DTI, 2000; Rahman *et al.*, 2000) it addresses the issues at a general level and with the understanding that in addition to any commonalities, all communities are different and distinct from each other.

The intention is to show the challenge that online learning faces to fulfil its potential in overcoming the barriers many people encounter when taking part in learning. The number of people who are perceived as being disadvantaged depends on the measurement criteria used. One important measure is income. There are 8.75 million people who live in households with less than 40 per cent of the average income (Rahman *et al.*, 2000).

The characteristics of a disadvantaged community are:

▶ many people are unemployed
▶ many people have been unemployed for several years
▶ there are considerable variations in patterns of unemployment between different groups who make up the community
▶ some deprived neighbourhoods have a high proportion of minority ethnic communities and in some cases a high proportion of people who have first languages other than English (DTI, 2000)
▶ a minority of families and individuals own a car
▶ few are self-employed
▶ the community suffers from high levels of crime
▶ the community suffers from poor long-term health
▶ households may be in temporary and uninsured accommodation
▶ few people have any qualifications
▶ there is little knowledge of the availability of learning opportunities
▶ many people will have had poor experiences of formal education
▶ many people have poor literacy, numeracy and language skills
▶ many people do not see the relevance of information and communication technologies (ICT) to their lives.

The major challenge for online learning in such a community is to convince the people within them that it is relevant and beneficial to them. This will mean different things to different people but will included providing people with skills and knowledge that will help them to find employment, enrich their lives and assist their children.

Adequate basic skills

The use of online learning requires people to have adequate basic skills. Almost all computer applications have been designed assuming users have good levels of English and in some cases Mathematics (e.g. spreadsheets). There are versions of many popular applications in most major languages for adults who speak English as a second language. However these are rarely available in learning centres or educational sites without specifically being purchased for a group or individual. This clearly hinders the possibilities of simply dropping into the centre. Perhaps equally important is that the internet largely uses the English language.

Online and computer-based learning have been shown to be powerful approaches to helping people develop basic skills. However, this requires the availability of tutors who are both competent computer users and who are also skilled in how to employ ICT in developing literacy numeracy and ESOL skills. Although it is difficult to measure at the moment, the majority of tutors are probably lacking ICT skills in both areas. There is considerable interest in this and efforts are being made to help tutors enhance their skills. The other barrier is that there are relatively few good quality ICT products designed to help develop basic skills.

Key conclusion

▶ The major challenge for online learning is to demonstrate its relevance to socially- and economically-disadvantaged adults.

7.2 Access to and use of the internet

Who uses the internet

By September 2000 (National Statistics) 45 per cent of adults had used the internet for a variety of reasons and 32 per cent of households had access to the internet from home. These figures are supported by the Whichonline Annual Internet Survey (2001) which reports 36 per cent of people have access to the internet. These two sets of results represent a rapid growth in home access over the previous 2 years. However this expansion may be short term. The Virtual Society (2000) programme's *Profile 2000* report stated that, 'the current rate of straightforward rapid expansion may not continue'.

The degree of access across Britain varies considerably from London (34%) to Northern Ireland (16%). There are similarly large differences in access relating to income, with 62 per cent of the highest earners having access compared to 7 per cent of the lowest incomes. These contrasts continue if we compare use by age with 82 per cent of those aged 16–24 having used the internet while only 14 per cent of those aged 65–74. Fifty-two per cent of men have used the internet compared to 39 per cent of women. Seventy-one per cent of professional households have used the internet compared to 26 per cent of unskilled households.

What this means

These statistics clearly describe the digital divide that has already been created in British society. This analysis is not new or limited to Britain. The Measuring Information Society (1997) survey considered the use of technology across Europe including Britain. It showed that the use of technology was related to age, gender and educational attainment. Adults aged over 55 years make less use of technology than younger groups, more men are information and communication technology (ICT) users or express an interest in technology than women, and adults who have received a higher level of education are more likely to use technology. The gap between men and women is closing with the Whichonline survey (2001) reporting that 45 per cent of internet users are women.

There have been a number of attempts to identify what use adults make of the internet. The IT for All surveys, covering 1996, 1997 and 1998, are shown in Table 3. The National Statistics survey (2000) shows a similar pattern of use and emphasis on the household, work-related activities, leisure, education and email. Two significant differences are that IT for All indicates a large interest over the years in education (59%; 65% and 73% respectively) and a relatively low use of email (10%; 19% and 30% respectively). The National Statistics survey showed a large interest in email (73% October 2000) with 36 per cent of users using their access to the internet solely for email while only 34 per cent reported using the internet for finding information about education. This difference is likely to be due simply to the question the users were asked or the interpretation of the word education, rather than anything significant. The email differences are more likely to be explained by a trend to use email identified in the IT for All surveys and that it takes a little time for a new user to be aware of value of email to them and also to locate other people with email accounts to write to. All these figures need to be considered in the light of the amount of access that an individual makes of the internet. The Whichonline survey (2001) reported that the majority of internet users only used it for less than 5 hours each week. It also suggested that access was often for locating information, education and research.

Table 3   Use of the home computer

Activity	1996	1997	1998
Personal/household	69%	78%	69%
Games	70%	70%	73%
Education	59%	65%	72%
Work brought home	54%	61%	61%
Hobbies	41%	41%	44%
Working from home	25%	28%	32%
Faxes	11%	22%	23%
Internet	10%	20%	32%
Email	10%	19%	30%

Anecdotal evidence is very evident about the value of email. Many tutors report considerable enthusiasm for communicating with students through email. It is not intrusive. They can send a message to a large number of students, provide access to themselves when the student has a question and support learners when away from the institution. In higher education email has become a major communication channel in less than a decade.

Sites of access

A key question is where did adults access the internet from and four locations dominate the responses (National Statistics, 2000):

▶ home   72%
▶ another person's home   34%
▶ workplace   38%
▶ educational location   24%.

This clearly shows the importance of personal ownership of the equipment or living in a community with many home computers, neither of which is likely to be true if you are poor or otherwise socially disadvantaged. Access to the internet through locations more accessible to people who are disadvantaged were also revealed. These included:

- library   7%
- cybercafe   9%
- community/voluntary organisation   1%.

The Government's UK Online Centres initiative is aiming to develop these types of locations for providing access to the internet. It is also worth considering the type of internet access that disadvantaged adults may have in their homes or local community. A type of digital divide can be encountered if your equipment is old or limited in functionality, speed and capacity. ICT equipment is continuously improving so individuals and communities need to be able to invest in their systems. Funding for ICT community centres is often short term while disadvantaged adults are unlikely to be able to make an initial investment, and a commitment to regular purchases is completely unrealistic.

Reasons for non-use

Fifty-five per cent of adults have not used the internet (National Statistics, 2000) for widespread reasons but four cover the vast majority:

- lack of interest   32%
- no need   22%
- lack of confidence/skills   21%
- cannot afford it   16%.

The IT for All surveys, in 1996, 1997 and 1998, identified groups of people who had some degree of doubt about the value of information technology (IT) to themselves. These groups were called unconvinced, concerned or alienated. Other studies have supported these findings (Measuring Information Society, 1997; IBM, 1997). In contrast several studies have suggested that there is enthusiasm from learners who are developing their ICT skills (Bissland, 1997; Clarke, 1998; IT for All, 1996). The conclusion is that there is a considerable need to make people aware of the value of ICT to themselves and once aware they are likely to be keen to become competent users.

The *IT Awareness Raising for Adults* report (Clarke, 1998) suggested that confidence building was a vital element in ICT courses since many adult learners see ICT as difficult to learn and doubt their own abilities to succeed. The national working party on social inclusion (IBM, 1997) recommend that 'measures are needed urgently to raise awareness and to provide access to information technologies, particularly for people on low incomes and for those who are neither in employment nor in education'. There are many initiatives underway both national and local to address the problem. However, the scale of the task is enormous with perhaps 20–30 million adults to reach.

Table 4 shows the relationship between access to the internet and current and future learning intention. It powerfully illustrates the link between the digital and learning divides.

Table 4 Participation in learning and future intention to learn, by access to the internet [1]

	Access to the internet	No access to the internet
Base (all respondents) = 100%	2,346	3,556
Current/recent participation in learning	67%	32%
Future intentions to learn	70%	35%

Key conclusion

▶ Access to ICT is dependent upon age, gender, geography, family, educational experience and income.
▶ There is a clear relationship between access to the internet and participation in learning.
▶ People with access to the internet use it for educational purposes.

1 Aldridge and Tuckett, 2001

7.3 *Learners' attitudes*

Research findings

The Campaign for Learning (2000) undertook three related surveys of employed e-learners, employers and learning providers. The e-learners had undertaken learning at work and at home; this had included both formal and informal activities. Informal learning was largely related to using the internet while formal activities were mainly linked to individuals working through learning material on their own. Learning material was either commercially purchased packs or material developed within the company.

E-learners stated that the main benefits were:

- convenience – learn at your own pace with rapid access to information
- keeping up-to-date
- satisfying individual interests and simple curiosity
- help with employment.

Employers believed that e-learning:

- improved access to learning
- reduced time spent away from the workplace
- could be individualised.

These are very similar to the perceived benefits of open and distance learning in general which is seen as being able to deliver learning at the place, pace and time to meet individual needs. To gain these outcomes is not easy and depends on combining many different factors into a learning programme. It is doubtful how successful workplace learning can be when the environment is noisy, stressful or distracting.

The big difference between online learning and other open learning approaches is that it allows a large dimension of informal learning using the vast resources of the internet and provides a powerful means of communication between individual learners and their tutors. It allows information to be found when it is needed assuming there is direct access to the internet. Few shop floor workers have access, many office workers still have limited access and many small- and medium-sized enterprises (SMEs) have no access.

Although most employees were positive towards e-learning many reservations were reported by the Campaign for Learning survey. These included that it was impersonal, frustrating and lonely to use and that materials were sometimes poor. The employees in the sample had almost universal access to the internet

(83% at work and 58% at home) and a high proportion had achieved degrees. A large proportion were from large organisations employing more than 500 people. SMEs are frequently less able to provide access to the internet or to training than larger organisations. This suggests that the sample did not include a substantial number of people who were socially- or economically-disadvantaged.

Participation in learning has been shown by many studies to relate to factors such as previous success in education, income and social class. Perhaps not surprisingly access to and use of computers is also related to similar factors.

The Department of Education and Employment (Clarke, 1998) undertook an investigation into effective approaches to becoming IT literate and identified three main factors which motivated adults to attend IT education and training courses. Analysis of the reasons for older learners to undertake information, communication and technology (ICT) courses in Leicestershire indicated a fourth reason (Ankers and Essom, 2000). These four reasons are:

▶ to assist their children's use of new technology
▶ to avoid being left behind by technological developments
▶ to obtain or hold a job
▶ curiosity and interest.

Table 5 shows the awareness in adults of new technologies compared to their perceived usefulness to them (IT for All, 1996; 1997). This shows that although adults are aware of the new technologies a large proportion did not feel they were relevant to their lives.

Table 5   Awareness and perceived usefulness of new technologies

Technologies	Awareness		Usefulness	
Base = 100% 3043				
	1996	**1997**	**1996**	**1997**
Personal computers (PC)	92%	93%	52%	57%
Internet	92%	96%	25%	34%
Modem	61%	71%	21%	26%
CD ROM	75%	84%	29%	36%

Table 6 shows the perceived usefulness of personal computers by age. The table compares the results of the two IT for All surveys (IT for All, 1996;1997). The major change has been a significant growth in the perceived usefulness of PCs for adult's aged 35–64. However, 50 per cent of 45–64 year olds still do not regard personal computers as being personally useful. The changes in the other age groups are minor.

Table 6   Personal perceived usefulness of personal computers

Age group	Perceived usefulness	
	1996	1997
Base = 100%	3043	3124
15–24	79%	76%
25–34	74%	72%
35–44	59%	72%
45–64	37%	50%
65+	22%	22%

Table 7 shows that the perceived usefulness of the internet has grown across all the age groups although the largest change has been in the age range 35–64. This reflects a similar pattern of growth in the perceived usefulness of the PC amongst the same age group.

Table 7   Perceived usefulness of the internet

Age group	Perceived usefulness	
	1996	1997
Base = 100%	3043	3124
15–24	54%	60%
25–34	36%	42%
35–44	22%	41%
45–64	14%	26%
65+	8%	10%

Large proportions of the population neither use technology nor are interested in it. This supports the results of the IT for All surveys (1996; 1998) and indicates that a major problem is simply motivating adults to see the relevance of technology to their own lives. National Statistics (2001) reported that 46 per cent of adults had never accessed the internet and of this group 41 per cent stated they had no interest in using the internet. This supports the IT for All results and shows that the issue of relevance of ICT to people's lives is not a short-term phenomenon. There are many millions of adults who are unlikely to take part in online learning due to being unable to perceive ICT as relevant to themselves.

Employment

There is considerable interest in the use of online learning amongst employers of all types and sizes. This is often related to factors such as:

- cost saving due to learning at the workplace
- just-in-time training (i.e. accessing segments of training immediately prior to needing the skills or knowledge)
- the ability to provide access to learning opportunities
- it is new, innovative and motivating.

These are very real potential benefits of online learning. However there are many practical issues to overcome such as:

- access
- support structure
- suitable learning materials.

Employers often suggest that the following skills are what they require from employees:

- computer literacy
- communication skills
- practical skills
- customer handling skills
- personal skills
- management skills
- literacy and numeracy skills.

The one that closely relates to online learning is computer literacy. A pre-requisite for online learning is that the learner is a competent ICT user. It has been suggested that a large proportion (90%) of new jobs require ICT skills or that a failure to become ICT literate is likely to be major barrier to employment and to accessing online learning in the workplace. This is a major limitation given the significance of the workplace as a site for learning activities (Sargant, 2000; DfEE, 1999). This analysis suggests that the lack of access to ICT and opportunities to become a competent ICT user that very disadvantaged adults encounter may both hinder their employment and their access to online learning.

Although computer-based learning materials and courses are limited, packages relating to ICT applications, skills and knowledge are widely available, many of them designed for use by employers. Their price and design makes their availability to individuals unlikely. One of the first commercial uses of online learning was to deliver professional updating to ICT consultants.

The price of change within ICT is illustrated by 60 per cent of applications being less than 2 years old and the life of ICT knowledge being less than 2 years. This shows the need for ICT users to be continuous learners, developing and revising their skills and knowledge. The internet provides an outstanding resource of information, learning materials and mail groups relating to the latest developments of ICT. Lack of access to these resources essentially denies learners a way of maintaining their skills. Many adults in disadvantaged communities have undertaken a basic ICT course often in the expectation that this will help them to gain employment. If this is not accompanied by an on-going effort to maintain and enhance these skills then the value will quickly be lost. Access to online resources is clearly an important route to developing ICT knowledge and skills.

Funding for lifelong learning in the community

Many initiatives are limited by short-term and partial funding. Although there are often a variety of projects underway in disadvantaged communities, they are often poorly linked or co-ordinated (Policy Action Team 15, 2000). ICT centres are now being established in many communities, but they are often limited or have no resources for long-term development. There is clearly a danger that although each centre will work hard and achieve good results, their overall impact will be limited due to a lack of sustained investment. A large amount of management time and resources is often devoted to fundraising rather than the direct work of the centre. Equally, funding bodies often require substantial evidence of achievement that can require centres to maintain records and employ staff on administration rather than primary tasks. A simple consideration of funding application processes reveals that in many cases it often requires a major investment in time and research which probably deters many small organisations from applying.

Learndirect are seeking to make links with community centres in order to establish them as access points for their network. This will provide adults with a progression route which is relatively straightforward. UK Online Centres have established a quality standard with an emphasis on centres providing a supportive environment for disadvantaged adults. Although Learndirect and UK Online Centres are to be welcomed and will make a positive contribution, there is still a great deal to be done.

Schools

Primary schools have been used extensively as locations for providing ICT courses in many parts of the country. They are excellent venues for adult learning if you are seeking to attract parents or grandparents of children attending the school. Head teachers are often enthusiastic about events which link their school with parents. Courses have been used to encourage learners to become volunteer helpers or classroom assistants. Equally, school staff have often taken part in courses to develop their own knowledge and skills.

The National Grid for Learning is providing every school with access to the internet and this would suggest that these are suitable locations for online learning. All the same there are significant barriers to this simple solution:

- security of the children
- conventional courses usually take place during school hours whereas online learning can happen at anytime. Opening a school in the evening has associated costs (e.g. care-taking, cleaning, electricity and telephone charges). Head teachers often do not have the funds to cover these costs
- school ICT equipment is configured for use by children and not for adults. Schools are naturally reluctant to allow their computers to be re-configured. It is doubtful if school equipment would be suitable for adults. Conventional ICT classes have been based on portable equipment bought in for the course.

A small number of schools have established community facilities which have the potential to overcome these barriers.

Individual issues

There are many issues which are needed to ensure the effectiveness of providing access to online learning. These include:

- adequate support both at the centre and online
- respect for learners as people at all parts of the process
- employment opportunities are a major motivation for many adults
- mentors who understand the needs of the learners
- tutors who can relate to the learners
- support after finishing the course to maximise its benefits or to progress to other opportunities
- quality learning materials ideally designed for adults returning to learning
- support for other learners, family and friends
- learning must be an enjoyable experience
- learners must be able to identify the benefit of learning for them
- learners must be able to choose what they learn
- support with developing their basic skills
- opportunities to plan ahead
- support with developing their online and other learning skills
- access to information, advice and guidance
- access for disabled people
- an acceptable location for accessing online resources and studying
- high quality standards for all aspects of the learning experience
- child or adult care arrangements are vital if parents/carers are able to take part.

This is a formidable list, but essential to ensure that adults returning to learning have an experience which makes them return for more and advocate the experience to their friends, family and peers. It contains many elements that would be recognised and shared by practitioners working in other areas of adult learning. The pedagogical thinking has much in common, so it is important not to let the technology, and its potential, divorce us from the wealth of knowledge and experience that underpins good practice elsewhere. There is a danger that this may happen since online learning can be seen as a quick solution to many deeply rooted problems.

Key conclusion

- Although many people are positive towards online learning there is a substantial minority who do not perceive that ICT is relevant to them.
- Although online learning is a new development it does have many features in common with traditional approaches.
- Online learning is not a quick fix.

7.4 Online communities

The potential of online communities

Online communities take many forms rather like physical ones. The major differences are that online communities are not limited by geography or time. It is possible for people in all parts of the world to communicate as easily as if they lived in the same street. Messages can be sent at any time and equally be read whenever it is convenient to the individual.

Groups who share a common interest or characteristic (e.g. age, hobby, health, shared experience, occupation or a problem) can be linked by communication technology no matter where the individuals reside. They are communities of interest. Academic communities were once restricted to a single campus but can now cover the whole world. Families scattered around the world can maintain their links through email as if they still lived in the same house. Ethnic minorities can maintain their languages and culture by connecting with each other and online newspapers.

Information and communication technologies (ICT) can play an important role in neighbourhood renewal (Shearman, 1999). A local website can act as a focus for bringing people together. Many villages, urban communities and groups have established websites serving many different purposes such as:

▶ acting as a newsletter for the community
▶ publishing creative material so local people can have their stories, poems and other art forms distributed
▶ linking local people to many sources of information.

A definition of online communities is offered by Preece (2001) who states that they consist of:

▶ people who interact socially as they strive to satisfy their own needs or perform special roles, such as leading or moderating
▶ a shared purpose, such as interest, need, information exchange or service, that provides a reason for the community to communicate
▶ policies, in the form of tacit assumptions, rituals, protocols, rules and laws that guide people's interactions
▶ computer systems to support and mediate social interaction and facilitate a sense of togetherness.

This shows the wide potential of online communities. They can take on many forms and serve a wide range of purposes. Conventional communities are often described in terms of their geographical area, population (e.g. age, gender, ethnic origin, etc.) and shared objectives. Individuals are often members of many different communities. Online communities are more difficult to describe since boundaries are often vague and ill defined. A group of people sharing a single hobby can be described as a community even though their interaction is limited to an occasional email message. Others are far more substantial with a wide range of shared aims, active co-operation and activities.

Online shopping, local and national Government and educational sites have the potential to create a form of community around each site. It is now possible to communicate with many Members of Parliament by email, send in your tax returns over the internet, purchase a wide range of products (e.g. books, music, holidays and cars) from websites. These are all manifestations of the development of a global online community.

Antwerp was one of the first cities in the world to create a form of virtual city for its population (Peeters, 2000). This was first launched in 1995 providing access to Government and cultural information but it has grown through offering individual email accounts and web space. It now integrates links between local hospitals, offers distance-learning opportunities, provides access to museums and libraries in the city and allows people to book services online. This is quite a modest set of developments compared to many forecasts of the future of online communities. However the city Government realised that it was vital to provide access and training to enable the citizens to take part and not be excluded from the virtual services. Antwerp provides:

▶ cybercafes providing free access to the internet
▶ nine cyberbuses
▶ free training courses
▶ information booths.

They are trying to overcome the key barriers of access to the technology and competence in using it.

Once people have overcome the barriers of access and competent use of the technology they are potentially equal online. They are invisible to other users and can present themselves in any way they want. It is difficult for other users to stereotype them or to discriminate against them. It is not possible, for example, to prevent people from sending messages as it is possible in a face-to-face environment to dominate a situation and stop others from contributing. As McConnell (2000) states, there is evidence to suggest that online conferences are more balanced in their contributions from men and women than face-to-face events.

Minority languages and culture can be supported with groups and individuals able to communicate with each other even when separated by thousands of miles. The SHUCAN project in Sheffield provided access for the community groups to the internet. The Yemani centre used the access to obtain copies of Middle Eastern Online newspapers to create a reading room. This contributed to maintaining the community's culture and language.

Families scattered around the world have discovered that email provides an effective means of keeping in-touch on a continuous basis. During the information technology (IT) awareness project (Clarke, 1998) access to email and the internet was provided to retirement homes in the Shetland Isles. Residents were able to communicate with their families in Canada and Australia exchanging photographs and chatting as if they still lived near to each other. This evidence suggests that older people are motivated to use ICT by the desire to talk to their families and friends, in a sense developing and supporting an extended online family.

Online communities can serve many purposes and one is to assist people to access learning. The mutual purpose of the internet was to help researchers to form an academic community. It would therefore seem appropriate to employ similar communities for learning, yet developing any community requires considerable effort and expertise and online communities are no different in this respect.

Key conclusion

▶ Communication technology allows new forms of community to be established and develop.
▶ ICT can aid the development of physical communities.
▶ Online communication is egalitarian.

7.5   *Informal learning*

Surfing the internet

One model of online learning is based on considering the internet as a gigantic library of information through which you can surf, finding the information and knowledge you need. This type of informal learning has the potential to reach many adults who have had poor experience of formal education and are reluctant to return to a course of study in an institutional setting. It does assume though that the learners are confident ICT users and are competent in searching for and judging the quality of information. These are advanced skills that a person returning to learning or new to the internet is unlikely to process.

McGivney (1999) identified a number of characteristics of informal learning and Table 8 shows how they relate to using the internet. It is clear that using the internet is a form of informal learning and has similar problems to other forms, such as judging the quality of the experience. Learning to use a computer and accessing the internet through informal methods has been shown to be effective. There is a potential to relate the two factors together so that the barrier of learning to use the internet as part of informal learning can be reduced.

All forms of informal learning are often difficult to accredit. Using the internet to learn a subject informally can potentially be accredited using the power of the computer to track information access and assessments undertaken online. There have been experiments to consider if accreditation can be carried without the learners being aware of the process so that the pressure of assessment does not affect them. This is possible but probably limited.

Search, locate and judge information

The main barrier to using the internet as a form of informal learning aside from the need to have access to the equipment and being a competent computer user, is the need to be able to search, locate and judge information provided on websites. At the moment anyone can launch a website and place online any information they choose. There are no widespread quality standards so the individual must be able to judge what they are reading and viewing in order to avoid being misled. Searching for and judging information are advanced skills which require time to develop and may prevent many people from benefiting from online resources. Nevertheless these skills are transferable to other aspects of life so they are in themselves useful to learn.

Table 8   Informal learning and the internet

Conventional	Internet
Often takes place in non-educational settings	Online resources can be accessed from many community locations and from people's homes
Location of learning is very important	Individuals can potentially learn anywhere that they find acceptable, including their homes
Many socially-disadvantaged people are attracted to informal learning opportunities	The internet is essentially a network of learning opportunities. However it does assume users are skilled in searching for and judging information and have access to the equipment. The cost of access is likely to be a significant barrier
Informal learning can help people gain self-confidence and self-esteem	Learning to use the computer in a community setting (Clarke, 1998) has been reported to have a similar effect
Informal learning can motivate people to progress in a variety of ways including more formal education	Learning to use the computer in a community setting (Clarke, 1998) has been reported to have similar effect

Key conclusion

▶ The internet is a useful means of aiding informal learning.

7.6 Teleworking

A growth area

Homeworking is often associated with poor pay, piecework and low status. The modern equivalent of teleworking has quite a different image. It is often the preserve of professionals or portfolio workers. The teleworker is attracted to homeworking for the same reasons as the traditional exploited adult. It is a convenient way of earning a living.

Teleworking is a growing activity either on a part-time or full-time basis. Many employers now provide access to their computer system from remote locations that allows individuals to occasionally or permanently work from home. In some cases this has been developed to allow for mobile access so that staff away from home are able to link to central systems through telephone connections. This growth in occasional or mobile teleworking is almost invisible in that the people taking part often do not regard themselves as teleworkers. Teleworking of this type is often linked to the changes in employment practice such as self-employment, fixed-term contracts, multiple employers and general flexible approaches to work.

This type of employment is often associated with particular sectors, sizes of employer and type of employment. Larger organisations are more likely to encourage part-time/mobile teleworking than small enterprises; professional and managerial staff rather than craft workers; and ICT-based (information and communication technology) companies rather than manufacturing. The nature of tasks undertaken is wide but includes research, sales, ICT (e.g. programming, data entry and design), secretarial and writing. A wide range of tasks are suitable for teleworking especially those involving the use of a computer or communication technology. It has grown rapidly in professional occupations.

Estimating the scale

The number of teleworkers is difficult to estimate due to problems of definition. It has been estimated, however, that the potential for teleworking in different types of employment within the UK is significant (Table 9). The actual numbers of current teleworkers are likely to be considerably lower than these potential figures. It is estimated that approximately 2 million people are engaged in employed and self-employed teleworking (EITO, 1998).

Table 9   Potential for teleworking

Occupation	Percentage of total workforce	
	1993	**2001**
Managers and administration	16.6%	19.8%
Professionals	9.1%	11.3%
Associate professionals/technical	9.3%	10.9%
Clerical/secretarial	16.2%	15.7%
Total	41.9%	57.7%
Total numbers (millions)	10.5	15.1

Using existing skills

For those who are constrained from taking a conventional job by family commitments, geography or other factors, teleworking is very attractive. However, it may not be an easy option to undertake unless they are already skilled in an area that is in demand.

Most part-time teleworking opportunities occur as a result of existing employment. Employers offer the possibility in order to maintain the employment of existing skilled workers. The Open University has several thousand part-time associate lecturers who work in many respects as teleworkers (i.e. many are evolving into online tutors). Nevertheless many associate lecturers are already employed and all have considerable expertise in a subject offered by the Open University.

Although this is an optimistic picture, teleworking is a new phenomenon and will change, expand and develop rapidly. Already companies send information to other continents for data processing so opportunities are almost certainly going to expand.

Online learning is an obvious way of providing support and training for teleworkers since they have access to the technology and are remote from training departments.

Key conclusion

▶ Teleworking is still developing.
▶ Online learning is a natural way of providing training for teleworkers.

7.7 *Digital democracy*

Universal access

The Government has committed itself to providing the population of Britain with universal access to the internet by 2005. What universal access means is not entirely clear but it almost certainly does not mean that every household will have its own computer, rather that a mixture of personal and public access will be available. This is likely to include:

- home computers
- public information and communication technology (ICT) centres
- public access through libraries
- public access through educational institutions
- mobile phone access
- digital television access.

This movement towards universal access is accompanied by a parallel development of allowing the individual to deal with the Government online. By 2001 approximately 33 per cent of Government department business is already online. By 2005 all elements that people interface with should be available to them in this way. Access to the internet will therefore assume an extra importance because it will also mean access to Government services. A lack of access may mean a reduction in access to the democratic process and the work of the Government.

Alienation

The other factor to consider is the willingness of people to use the internet. The IT for All surveys (1996; 1997) indicate a substantial part of the population (approximately 20%) have a very poor view of the internet to the extent that the surveys identified them as 'alienated'. This was confirmed by the Consumer Association survey (2000) that showed that a significant proportion of the population believed that the internet was irrelevant to their lives. This suggests that simple access is not enough but that many people need to be convinced that the internet is useful to them. They are unlikely to take part in the initiatives undertaken by the Government and others (e.g. the BBC) such as IT for All, UK Online, Computer's Don't Bite and Webwise, since these assume at least a willingness to undertake a taster experience.

At the moment many socially- or economically-disadvantaged people are forced to shop in small local shops that charge higher prices than out of town supermarkets. They are effectively disadvantaged by not having a car and the lack of access to the internet is also likely to bring about similar practical disadvantages. They will not have straightforward access to Benefit services, NHS advice services and educational resources. This may result in their lives being made poorer.

The exclusivity of online citizenship

Already many Members of Parliament have their own websites and provide an email address through which they can be contacted. This is clearly an important development since it increases the potential of communication between the individual citizen and their representative. Without access to and understanding of how to use email the individual is denied this important communication route. Email is also the means of allowing the individual to talk to others with similar interests so that ideas, common concerns and interests can be shared. This allows geographically remote people to develop a new form of community so that they can effectively take part in democratic actions. In the USA there have already been several examples of candidates using the internet to campaign for office without the normal party infrastructure.

The move to make government services and information more accessible is to be welcomed, but if some parts of the country do not have access we will be adding to the exclusion. It is very likely that in parallel with the development of online services will be a rationalisation of physical access where people will have substantially less access if they are not able to use online facilities.

Key conclusion

▶ As the democratic forms migrate to the online world it is likely that socially-excluded groups will be further disadvantaged.

7.8 Access to knowledge

Social exlusion and the digital divide

Many millions of words have been written and spoken about the knowledge economy. It is sufficient to repeat that adults who are not competent users of information and communication technologies (ICT) and skilled in using communication technologies will be increasingly disadvantaged in obtaining and keeping employment. Also with the growth in online learning they will be excluded from some key learning opportunities.

There is another issue. With escalating amounts of information available online, adults will be increasingly at a disadvantage if they do not have access to the internet in their normal everyday lives. People who have been using the internet automatically seek answers to their questions online. It can help with many issues such as:

- children's homework
- shopping
- travel
- finances
- benefits and tax.

Families who do not have access will be disadvantaged and will be in danger of passing their disadvantage on to their children. Social exclusion is a multi-faceted issue of which the digital divide is only one aspect. It is one that can both help to overcome some of the other components of disadvantage but can also add to exclusion.

7.9 Barriers to online learning

Types of barrier
The barriers to online learning can be divided into four groups:

- barriers for learners who are socially- or economically-disadvantaged
- barriers for tutors
- barriers for organisations
- barriers for communities.

Learners
Adults who are socially- or economically-disadvantaged face a variety of barriers. These include:

- access to information and communication technologies (ICT)
- a lack of suitable online learning materials which have been specifically designed for adults returning to learning
- a lack of trained tutors and support staff
- individuals having a lack of:
  - confidence in their ability to learn
  - motivation
  - incentive
  - basic skills
  - ICT basic skills
- the cost to the individual of accessing the internet, buying equipment and telephone charges
- standard technology unsuitable for learners with special needs and limited understanding of adaptations.

Tutors
Tutors also face barriers in using online learning. These include:

- a lack of expertise in ICT
- a lack of expertise in how to employ ICT in learning
- a limited understanding of the needs of disadvantaged learners
- a limited experience in developing online study skills
- personal attitudes and approaches to learning. These are complex but include tutors who will see online approaches as a threat to their established skills and experience.

Organisations

Educational institutions face many barriers to providing and supporting online learning. These include:

- attitudes of existing educational institutions and their staff towards online learning. Change is often not welcomed by organisations especially when it challenges well-established structures
- the cost of the investment in online facilities, materials and staff development. This is not simply the initial costs but the depreciation charges to allow for the rapidly changing nature of technology and materials
- a lack of understanding of ICT/online learning amongst decision-makers (e.g. potential, knowledge, approach, costs, benefits)
- an organisational unwillingness to change structures to accommodate online learning
- a limited range of online courses and quality materials
- a limited number of staff with the skills to create high quality online learning materials and courses
- a limited number of staff with online tutoring and support skills.

Other non-educational organisations also need to overcome barriers to provide online learning to their employees. These include:

- access to ICT for all staff. Currently only professional and office staff have desktop computers and many are not linked to the internet. Shop floor workers sometimes have no easy access to technology
- a limited availability of mentors, coaches and other support staff for people taking part in online learning
- an organisational culture which does not see learning as a priority.

Communities

Communities have to overcome a range of barriers to provide online learning to their people. These include:

- access to ICT in community locations acceptable to adults who are socially excluded
- limited local experience or understanding of online learning
- limited online materials and courses designed for socially-excluded people
- limited online learning materials in minority ethnic languages
- a population who do not see the relevance of ICT to their lives
- many people with limited confidence and self-esteem.

Key conclusion

- To successfully introduce online learning requires a wide range of factors to be addressed. These factors relate to the individual, the tutor, the organisation and the community.

7.10 ICT and the family

Helping the children

A number of surveys have indicated that a powerful motivator for adults to learn about information and communication technologies (ICT) is to help their children (Clarke, 1998; IT for All, 1996; 1997; National Statistics, 2000). This is demonstrated in particular by the tendency for families with children to own their own computers and to have access to the internet. The potential for home learning has not been investigated in depth even though it is probably growing faster than the use of computers in school (Wellington, 2001). The use of home computers has generated some widely held anecdotes about how families use ICT. These include:

- children's use of ICT to aid their learning encourages their parents, in some cases their grandparents, to use it for similar purposes
- parents use of ICT to aid their learning encourages their children to use it for similar purposes.

Keeping in touch with extended family

Older learners often describe their reasons for using ICT in terms of communicating with their extended family. This is perhaps a key reason in a society were families are often separated by considerable distances. Email provides the means for families staying in daily contact, sharing photographs of growing grandchildren and ensuring elderly parents are well.

Adult and Community Learning Laptop Initiative

During the Adult and Community Learning Laptop Initiative voluntary and community organisations were provided with modern laptops in order to assist them provide learning opportunities to local communities. Over 300 organisations took part in the initiative and many reported that the computers played a key role in:

- motivating adults
- aiding family learning
- taking learning into people's homes
- providing access to ICT for tenants' groups
- influencing the practice of adult tutors who work with families.

Researching the use of computers in the home

Computers have a role in providing learning within the home, however it is not clear how a family interacts with computers and online learning resources. Does

ICT generate family learning or simply individual learning in the home? During 2000/2001, NIACE on behalf of Leicestershire Training and Enterprise Council undertook an investigation into how computers were used within households. This involved interviews with 56 adults (39 women and 17 men) from 51 households. The average age of the participants was 50.6 years old but a wide range of people were involved. This included:

▶ 1 interviewee aged under 25
▶ 9 interviewees aged 25–34
▶ 10 interviewees aged 35–44
▶ 12 interviewees aged 45–54
▶ 10 interviewees aged 55–64
▶ 14 interviewees aged 65–74.

The households involved included:

▶ 8 single adult households
▶ 3 lone parents with children
▶ 14 adult couples with children
▶ 26 adult couples with no children living in the households.

The interviewees included 13 in part-time and 13 in full-time employment, 20 retired and 10 not in paid employment. Ten people did not have access to ICT in their homes while 46 had home computers and 37 had access to the internet as well. The motivation for obtaining access to ICT covered a range of issues and were related to:

▶ improving job prospects (7%)
▶ previous experience of using ICT (11%)
▶ for use by other members of the family (17%)
▶ in order to gain access to the internet (14%)
▶ to help develop ICT skills and knowledge (27%)
▶ to communicate (e.g. email) (10%)
▶ for use within the household (10%)
▶ for work (4%).

Interviewees often gave multiple reasons for their use of ICT but the largest single factor being related to a general interest. This may be linked to the age range of the sample, with a greater number of older people, and this would correspond with Ankers and Essom's (2000) report on reasons why older learners take ICT courses. The participants were also asked about what use they put the home computer to and their responses were again widespread:

▶ community activities (8%)
▶ paid work (6%)
▶ household activities (12%)
▶ studying and skills development (7%)
▶ developing ICT skills (6%)
▶ letter writing (4%)
▶ hobbies and interests (8%)

- school work and children's education (10%)
- games (11%)
- job applications (less than 1%)
- email (14%)
- internet (13%).

The participants' use of the internet was probed and revealed six main uses:

- shopping (28%)
- travel and holidays (22%)
- hobbies and interests (20%)
- children's education (9%)
- finance (8%)
- other (13%).

The 'other' category includes professional development, website development, access to news, access to medical information and job searching. There were also many responses that stated or implied that they used the internet as a sort of reference library. In a sense the internet was being used for a type of informal learning. This is reinforced by the other answers, with a fifth of the sample using it to develop hobbies and interests.

The participants were asked specifically about online learning, revealing a positive attitude. Sixty-six per cent of the interviewees would be interested in using online learning. They would be interested in taking part in courses, which were related to:

- personal interests (49%)
- work-related (24%)
- developing ICT skills and knowledge (27%).

This is a small study and the participants are clearly not representative of the whole population but it does show some positive attitudes to the use of online learning for both vocational and other learning including both formal courses and more informal learning.

The National Statistics surveys (2000) reveal a similar picture of internet use with a large interest in using it for shopping or related activities, financial matters and general surfing to find information which is frequently linked to education. This tends to support the view that people are interested and actively using the internet for learning. The IT for All surveys (1996; 1999) showed a consistent use of ICT for educational activities.

When the Leicestershire sample were asked what were the advantages of using online learning they stated that:

- it would allow them to study at a time which suited them (42%)
- it would allow them to study at a pace they preferred (9%)
- it would be cheaper (3%)
- it would help fit studying into their domestic circumstances (46%).

This shows that this group understands the benefits of online learning.

Key conclusion

- Our understanding of how ICT impacts on a family and its relationships is not complete. However, there is a link between families with children and ICT ownership.
- There is a need for more research into ICT and the family.

7.11 ICT in the community

Community regeneration

There are several examples of how the use of information and communication technologies (ICT) can help to regenerate communities by providing a tool to bring people together, motivate them and assist them with increasing the availability of learning opportunities. Nevertheless, it is essentially still true to suggest that (Fabian Society, 2001):

- many disadvantaged adults do not have access to ICT
- professionals do not have a clear understanding of how ICT can assist with neighbourhood renewal.

In 1998, the Department for Education and Employment launched the Adult and Community Laptop initiative that involved the distribution of 1500 modern internet-ready laptop computers to Local Authority Adult Education Services and to community and voluntary organisations. The overall aim was to provide the technology to deliver learning into the community with an emphasis on reaching adults who are socially- or economically-disadvantaged.

Eighteen months into the initiative the organisations were surveyed about their use of the equipment, 129 organisations returned a completed questionnaire (Aldridge 2001).

Research findings

Figure 1 provides an overview of the use of the laptops, which shows the widespread use of the technology. The two major areas being ICT and basic skills but with many other significant uses including staff development, developing learning materials and youth work. The laptops were used in both formal and informal learning with most organisations adopting a flexible approach, maximising the potential of working in the community at locations acceptable to the learners.

Figure 1   Overall laptop use

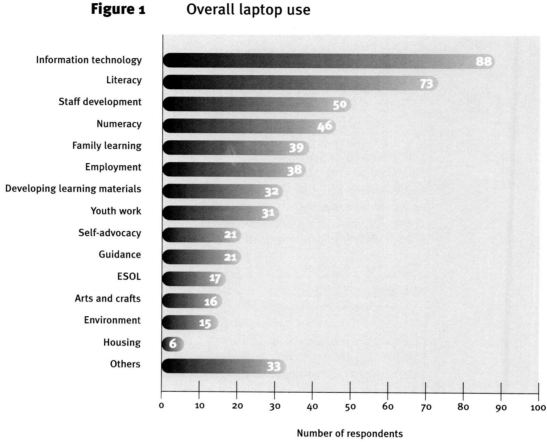

Number of respondents

This range of subjects indicates that the use of technology can facilitate learning across a wide range of subjects and needs.

Figure 2 shows the breakdown of locations used. The locations mentioned included day centres, resource centres, museums, residential care centres, public houses, churches, probation hostels and youth clubs. This clearly shows the potential for online or technology-based learning to overcome the barrier of place. The simple of use of portable equipment allows learners to access learning at locations where they are comfortable.

Figure 2   Location of use

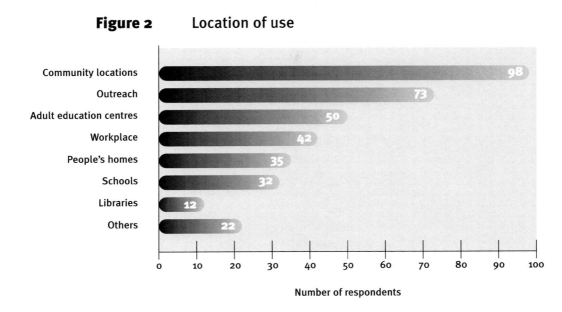

Number of respondents

Organisations were asked to estimate how much of their work was aimed at widening participation. This provides an estimate that 70 per cent of the work within the laptop initiative concentrated on widening participation. Figure 3 shows an analysis of the learners who took part in the initiative. This shows the wide range of people who were reached by the use of technology and demonstrates the potential of technology to engage many groups who often do not take part in learning.

Figure 3   Who are the learners?

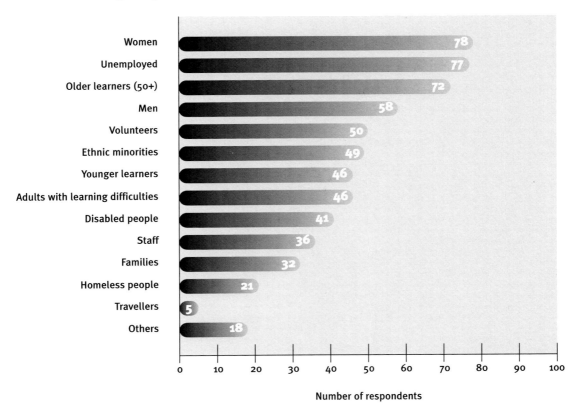

Number of respondents

Voicing the potential

Although this evidence is drawn from a single initiative it is large scale and clearly focused in the community in order to reach socially- and economically-disadvantaged adults. Some quotes from organisations illustrate the potential of technology-based learning:

'[It] allowed us to reach out to rural areas of the county and deliver training to those who are isolated from adult education centres.'

'Seventy-five per cent of our learners do not own their own computer equipment. The facility to use the laptops on a drop-in basis has been crucial to them over the last 12–18 months.'

'The laptop programme has enabled us to offer more courses at community venues. Students are attracted by [the] IT component. [It is] also beneficial in building confidence in IT skills so students will more readily consider moving on to college-based programmes.'

Key conclusion

▶ ICT can contribute to providing a wide range of learning in community settings.
▶ There is still much to be learned about employing ICT in communities.

7.12 ICT and the learner

Personal use of ICT

This section is key to the whole publication as information and communication technologies (ICT) and social exclusion relates to the use of ICT by individuals and their learning. This section considers the personal use of ICT rather than the more global aspects considered elsewhere. There are many ways of using and learning about ICT. They can be grouped in terms of:

- presenting information (e.g. word processing, spreadsheets, charts and graphs, desktop publishing and drawing applications)
- finding information (e.g. databases and the internet)
- manipulating information (e.g. word processing and spreadsheets)
- communicating (e.g. email, chat, conferencing and group work).

It is a formidable list and it is important not to underestimate the challenge ICT presents to a learner. To an individual who is returning to learning after a long break it is a large barrier. ICT is often considered to be difficult to learn and, although major efforts have been made to create user-friendly applications, they are still a considerable distance from this goal.

Personal development

A key issue is that ICT is continuously changing, developing and expanding so that learners need to undertake an informal programme of self-development to maintain their skills and knowledge. This requires them transferring their existing understanding to new situations and carrying out their own self-development.

The main emphasis in current basic ICT courses is on helping individuals to become competent users of particular applications. There is little emphasis on developing a deeper, more structural understanding of ICT or in helping learners transfer their knowledge and skills to new situations. This is likely to produce learners who may find even a new version of an application they are able to use, a challenge.

Many adults who take part in basic ICT courses do not own a computer or have access to ICT outside of the course. ICT is a practical subject that requires practice to both develop and maintain. There is a real danger that successful ICT learners may gradually lose their skills and knowledge if they are not able to practice. This is particularly true in ICT due to the rapid development of the subject.

Limitations of public access

Public access to ICT is improving with many thousands of ICT centres offering access to individuals, being made available. These are not always free even when they are sited in a public organisation such as a library. Even a small charge is a barrier.

Also important is whether people's use of a public resource is similar to how they would use a private one. Using the internet requires learners who are confident enough to browse the content, make decisions about quality and availability as well as selecting search criteria to locate the desired information. Earlier research has indicated that this type of use is associated with confident learners (Clarke, 1996). For learners who are trying to develop their skills, perhaps with a lack of confidence and awareness of the cost of access, a public facility may be very limiting. Clarke (1998) reported that the structure and support in centres was critical to avoid learners dropping out.

ICT skills and knowledge are key skills within the information society. For online learning they are essential before learners take advantage of its benefits.

Key conclusion

▶ Learners must be competent and confident users of ICT in order to take advantage of online learning.

7.13 ICT in the organisation

The impact of ICT in the workplace

The impact of information and communication technologies (ICT) on almost all organisations has been dramatic. Over the last 15 years it has significantly changed many – few have remained unaltered. ICT is a core skill for employability and many organisations have made substantial investment in the training of their employees. However access to ICT is often segregated within organisations with professional, administrative and clerical staff having individual computers and frequent email and internet access. Shop floor workers often do not have access except through a learning centre with limited opportunities to use it. Due to this pattern, opportunities to employ online learning are also likely to be limited.

George and Cooper (2001), reporting on an investigation of the use of computer-based learning, showed that these methods are used for management training far more than the training of other staff. Computer-based training was far more likely to be available in large organisations rather than small ones.

The organisations that used computer-based learning identified the following benefits:

- flexibility
- cost-effectiveness
- reliability
- concentrates on meeting the needs of people.

There were worries about learner isolation, providing sufficient support and maintaining progress.

These results tend to follow the pattern for the provision of all forms of training. Managers and office staff are more likely to be provided with off-the-job training than shop floor staff. Rahman *et al.* (2000) reported that people with qualifications were three times more likely to receive job-related training than those without qualifications. Online learning therefore is not immediately overcoming the barriers which lower paid manual workers face in accessing training. It is simply following the established patterns.

Restrictions to ICT development

Access to the internet from individual personal computers is often restricted by organisations. In some cases, searching the internet is identified with playing or non-productive activities. This is disappointing given the increasing need for employees to be confident users of ICT. These limitations have been extended by the real fears of virus attack or litigation if an employee sends a critical email. The overall effects are to limit the opportunities to explore ICT in order to enhance and maintain their skills and knowledge.

Although many organisations adopted ICT several years ago, for others, in particular small- and medium-sized enterprises (SMEs), it is a recent development. They are still in the process of introducing ICT so that they often do not have an integrated infrastructure in place. This reduces the opportunities available for SME employees to develop or practice their ICT skills, and at the moment it is unlikely that many could take part in online learning without significant external support.

A final issue for all organisations is the ICT skill shortage which has effected all parts of the country. Online learning requires a sound technical structure combined with learners who are confident users of ICT. There are very few people with ICT qualifications in the workforce (Learning and Skills Council, 2001). The shortage of ICT skills influences both areas in that learners often lack confidence and organisations are often careful to avoid increasing pressures on existing professional staff with new ICT developments. Anecdotal evidence suggests that a lack of technical assistance is a critical factor in learners being dissatisfied with online learning.

Key conclusion

▶ Online learning has been identified by many organisations as a way of providing training for employees. However, many organisations do not have the infrastructure to support online approaches.

8 Conclusions and recommendations

Online learning clearly has considerable potential to overcome many of the barriers encountered by adults who are socially or economically disadvantaged when taking part in learning. However it is not a panacea to solve all problems. Adults are frequently disadvantaged in many ways so online learning faces a significant challenge to realise its potential. It is very new and the main sources of evidence about good practice come from contexts significantly different from an adult returning to learning after many years or with poor previous experience of education.

There is a great deal to be done to investigate and understand the effective use of online learning. The speed at which it has been introduced and is growing makes it almost impossible for researchers to carry out and publish their work before new technological developments are launched. This should be seen as an incentive to undertake research since the underpinning learning issues tend not to change just because the technology does.

In order for the potential of online learning to be realised, many separate and in some cases related actions need to be undertaken. We therefore offer the following recommendations:

- Online learning skills – to be a successful online learner requires high quality learning skills. Online courses need to be designed to assist the development of learning skills.
- Design of materials – there are relatively few high quality online learning materials that have been specially designed for returning learners or to aid the development of learning skills. Materials are needed that are specifically designed for adults returning to learning.
- Training of designers – there are few opportunities to receive training as an online learning designer. A national training programme is required to ensure that online learning designers are not in short supply.
- Training of online tutors – although several training courses have become available, it is not entirely clear the basis on which they are designed. A review and comparison of the different approaches would be useful to identify their strengths and weaknesses to support returning learners.
- People will require a combination of outreach activities, mentoring and tutorial support to encourage them to take advantage of online learning.
- There is a need for staff development in:
  - outreach, mentoring and support in community settings for staff skilled in online learning
  - online learning and perhaps information and communication technologies (ICT) in general for staff with experience of working in the community
  - online tutoring and support skills.

- Although it is not a solution to all problems, technology can provide many aids to help adults overcome physical barriers to participating. For the technology to be used effectively requires:
  - more research and development to turn potential into reality
  - training for tutors to understand the nature and existence of current solutions
  - training for designers of online materials and websites to understand how to design products which allow access solutions (e.g. screen readers) to work.
- Retention – retention is a major issue with a substantial risk that many learners will fail to complete online courses. There is a need to identify and understand the factors that lead to an individual dropping out and completing the course.
- Research evidence – a large volume of the research evidence on which online learning approaches are based, was identified in higher education or contexts other than disadvantaged adults. There is a need to review the findings to identify their applicability for adults returning to learning.
- First steps – the use of laptops and other portable equipment has been shown to be an effective approach to encouraging disadvantaged adults to start to gain ICT skills and understanding. The good practice available in many locations across the country needs to be distilled into a series of guides.
- Disadvantaged adults need to be shown why ICT is relevant to their lives. There are many initiatives and projects that are working in this area. The good practice needs to be identified, distilled and made available.
- ICT in the family – there is little longitudinal evidence available on the use of ICT within a household. We would recommend that research be undertaken.
- Online learning must be related to and integrated with community developments to provide an environment in which learners are supported to take part in learning and to be successful learners.
- The speed of implementation is very fast so it is vital that the emerging evidence, good practice and ideas are effectively disseminated to practitioners to allow them to take advantage of them.

References

Fiona Aldridge, F (2001) *DfES Laptop Initiative for Adult and Community Learning: Summary results from the 18 month survey,* unpublished report to the Department for Education and Employment, NIACE

Aldridge, F and Tuckett, A (2001) *Winners and Losers,* NIACE

Ankers, A and Essom, J (2000) *ICT and Older Learners,* unpublished report for Leicestershire TEC, NIACE

Arenicola Designs (2000) *Authoring for CBT and Interactive Multimedia,* Lifelong Learning and Technology Division, Department for Education and Employment

BASE: www.base.odl.org/controlE.html

BSA and University for Industry (2000) *Getting Better Skills: What motivates adults,* Basic Skills Agency

BECTA (2001) *The 'Digital Divide': A discussion paper,* unpublished paper, British Education Communication Technology Agency

Bissland, V (1997) *Easy for Some: Attitudes to learning in later life students to learning computer skills,* Senior Studies Institute, University of Strathclyde

California Distance Learning Project (1997) *What is Distance Education?* www.cdlponline.org

Campaign for Learning (2000) *Attitudes to E-Learning,* Campaign for Learning

Carey, J (1999) *Joined Up Citizenship: ICT and disabled people,* Department of Trade and Industry

Clarke, A (1996) *Principles of Screen Design for Computer-Based Learning materials,* unpublished thesis, University of Sheffield

Clarke, A (1998) *IT Awareness Raising for Adults,* Department of Education and Employment, OL 254

Clarke, A (1998) unpublished report of COCODIS Socrates Project

Clarke, A (1999) *Learning Centres,* unpublished report for Hackney Adult Education Service

Clarke, A (2000) *Learning Organisations: What they are and to become one,* NIACE

Clarke, A (2001) *Evaluation Report Can-Do Project,* unpublished report into ADAPT/UFI project, NIACE

Clarke, A and Walmsley, J (1999) *Open Learning Materials and Centres,* NIACE

Collis, B and Meeuwsen, E (1999) 'Learning to Learn in a WWW-based Environment', in *Internet Based Learning* edited by French, D, Hale, C, Johnson, C, *et al.* (1999) Kogan Page

Consumer Association Survey (2000) *Annual Internet Survey,* Which Online www.which.net/surveys/findings.htm

Crowley-Bainton, T (1995) *Evaluation of the Open Learning Credits Pilot Programme: Summary report,* Policy Studies Institute, Department of Employment, Research Series No. 45

DfEE (1999) *Pathways in Adult Learning,* Department for Education and Employment

DTI (2000), *Closing the Digital Divide: Information and communication technologies in deprived areas,* Department of Trade and Industry, PAT 15

Doring, A (1999) 'Information Overload? The Learner and the Internet: A source of knowledge or too much of a good thing?' in *Adults Learning,* 10(10)

EITO (1998) *European Information Technology Observatory 1998,* European Information Technology Observatory

Epic Group (2000) *Taking Training On Line,* Lifelong Learning and Technology Division, Department for Education and Employment

Fabian Society (2001) *Beyond Access: ICT and social inclusion, summary of Fabian Society report and recommendations,* Fabian Society www.fabian-society.org.uk

Foshay, R (ed) (1994) *Effectiveness of Computer-Based Training: An annotated bibliography of reviews 1980–1993,* TRO Learning www.plato.com/papers/pdf/training.pdf

Freenberg, A (1998) 'Distance Learning: Promise or Threat?', *Crosstalk,* Winter www-rohan.sdsu.edu/faculty/freenberg/TELE3.HTM

French, D, Hale, C, Johnson, C *et al.* (1999) *Internet-based learning,* Kogan Page

FEFC (2000) *Open and Distance Learning, National Report from the Inspectorate 2000–01,* Further Education Funding Council

Fuller, D, Norby, R, Pearce, K, *et al.* (2000) 'Internet Teaching by Style: Profiling the online professor' in *Education Technology and Society,* 3(2)

Future.com (1997) 'UK attitudes to New Technology', in *Moving into the Information Society: An international benchmarking study,* Department of Trade and Industry

George, A and Cooper, C (2001) *Employers' Use and Awareness of Vocational Learning Approaches,* Department for Employment and Education, Research Report 246

GHK Economics and Management (1998) *IT Labour Market Assessment: A review of available information,* Department for Education and Employment

Great Britain National Skills Task Force (2000) *Skills for All: Proposals for a national skills agenda: Final report of the National Skills Task Force,* Department for Education and Employment

Harasim, L, Hiltz, SR, Teles, L *et al.* (1995) *Learning Networks: A field guide to teaching and learning online,* MIT Press

IBM (1996) *Social Exclusion, Technology and the Learning Society, Living in the Information Society,* IBM

IBM (1997) *The Net Result: Social Inclusion in the Information Society, Report of the National Working Party on Social Inclusion (INSINC),* Corporate Affairs, IBM

Jung, I (2000) 'Distance Education in Korea', *Open Learning,* 15(3), 217–231

IT for All (1996) *A survey into Public Awareness of, Attitudes Towards, and Access to Information and Communication Technologies,* Department of Trade and Industry

IT for All (1997) *The Latest Findings Concerning Attitudes Towards IT,* Department of Trade and Industry

IT for All (1998) *The Latest Findings Concerning Attitudes Towards IT,* Department of Trade and Industry

Hara, N and Kling, R (2000) 'Student Distress in a Web-Based Distance Education Course' in *Information, Communication and Society,* 3(4)

Hunt, M and Clarke, A (1997) *A Guide to the Cost-Effectiveness of Technology-Based Training,* Department for Education and Employment

Khan, BH (1997) *Web-Based Instruction (WBI): An introduction,* Educational Technology Publications

Learning Methods Project (1993) Department for Education and Employment

LSC (2001), *Partnership to Drive up E-Skills,* Press Release, Learning and Skills Council

LSDA (2001), *Agency Responds: Skills for life,* Learning and Skills Development Agency

Mager, C (2000) *FEDA responds to National Strategy for Neighbourhood Renewal,* FEDA

Maynard, S (1998) *Hackney Lifelong Learning Research,* Maynard and Associates

McConnell, D (2000) *Implementing Computer–Supported Cooperative Learning, 2nd Edition,* Kogan Page

McGivney, V (1996) *Staying or Leaving the Course,* NIACE

McGivney, V (1999) *Informal Learning in the Community,* NIACE

McGivney, V (2000) *Recovering Outreach: Concepts, practices and issues,* NIACE

McManus, TF (1995) 'Delivering Instruction on the World Wide Web', in *Teaching and Learning* by Litchfield, A (ed) (1996) Electronic Document
www.ccwf.cc.utexas.edu/~mcmanus/special.htm

EU (1997) *Measuring Information Society: A survey based on 15,900 face-to-face interviews,* EU

www.ispo.cec.be/infosoc/promo/pubs/poll97/eurabaroen.htm

MORI (1999) *Rage Against the Machine,* Compaq Computers Ltd
www.compaq.co.uk/rage

MORI (2000) *Getting Better Basic Skills – What Motivates Adults,* Basic Skills Agency

National Skills Task Force (2000) *Skills for All: Proposals for a national skills agenda: Final report of the National Skills Taskforce,* DfEE

National Statistics (2000) *Internet Access,* Family Expenditure Survey

Neilson, J (2000) *Designing Web Usability,* New Riders Publishing

Ng, K (2000) 'Cost-Effectiveness of Online Courses, *Open Learning,* 15(3), 300–308

NIACE (2000) *Mailgroup,* Briefing Sheet, NIACE

Nipper, S (1989) 'Third Generation Distance Learning and Computer Conferencing' in *Mindweave: Communication, computers and distance education* by Mason, R and Kaye, A (eds) (1989) Pergamon Press

Nonnecke, B and Preece, J (2000) *Lurker Demographics: Counting the silent,* CHI 2000 conference proceedings, ACM Press

NOP (1997) *State of the Nation Research Findings: An in-depth look at Britain's attitudes towards technology,* Microsoft

OECD (1996) *Technology, Productivity and Jobs,* OECD

OFTEL (2000) *Consumers' Use of the Internet,* OFTEL
www.oftel.gov.uk/cmu/research/into800.htm

Owston, RD (1997) 'The World Wide Web: A technology to enhance teaching and learning?', *Educational Researcher,* 26, 27–33

Palloff, RM and Pratt, K (1999) *Building Learning Communities in Cyberspace: Effective strategies for the online classroom,* Jossey-Bass Publishers

Petre, M, Carswell, L, Price, B *et al.* (2000) 'Innovations in Large-Scale Supported Distance Teaching: Transformation for the internet, not just translation', in *The Knowledge Web,* Eisenstadt, M and Vincent , T (eds) Kogan Page

Peeters, B (2000) 'The Information Society in the City of Antwerp', in *Digital Cities,* Ishida, T and Isbister, K (eds) (2000), Springer

Policy Action Team 15 (2000) *Closing the Digital Divide: Information and communication technologies in deprived areas,* Department for Trade and Industry

Preece, J (2001) *Online Communities,* Wiley

Rahman, M, Palmer, G, Kenway, P *et al.* (2000) *Monitoring, Poverty and Social Exclusion 2000,* New Policy Institute, Joseph Rowntree Foundation

Reeves, TC and Reeves, PM (1997) 'Effective Dimensions of Interactive Learning on the World Wide Web', in *Web-Based Instruction,* Khan, BH (ed), Educational Technology Publications

Russell, N and Drew, N (2001) *ICT Access and Use,* Research Brief 252, Department for Education and Employment

Rojo, A and Ragsdale, RG (1997) 'A Process Perspective on Participation in Scholarly Electronic Forums', *Science Communication,* 18(4), p320–341

Salmon, G (2000) *E-Moderating,* Kogan Page

Sargant, N (2000) *The Learning Divide Revisited,* NIACE

Sargant, N, Field, J, Francis, H, *et al.* (1997), *The Learning Divide: A study of participation in adult learning in the United Kingdom,* NIACE

Sharan, S (1990) *Cooperative Learning: Theory and research,* Praeger

Simpson, O (2000) *Supporting Students in Open and Distance Learning,* Kogan Page

Shearman, C (1999) *Local Connections: Making the net work for neighbourhood renewal,* Communities Online

Slavin, RE (1990) Cooperative Learning: *Theory, research and practice, Prentice Hall*

Social Exclusion Unit (2001) *A New Commitment to Neighbourhood Renewal: National Strategy Action Plan,* Cabinet Office

Stefanov, K, Stoyanov, S and Nikolov, R (1998) 'Design Issues of a Distance Learning Course on Business on the Internet' in *Journal of Computer-Assisted Learning 14(2)*

Tait, A (2000) 'Planning Student Support', *Open Learning,* 15(3), 287–299

Tolley, S (2000) 'How Electronic Conferencing Affects Teaching', *Open Learning,* 15(3), 253–265

Virtual Society (2000) *Virtual Society? The social science of electronic technologies. Profile 2000,* Economic and Social Research Council

Weller, MJ (2000) 'Creating a Large-Scale, Third Generation, Distance Education Course', *Open Learning,* 15(3), 241–252

Wellington, J (2001) 'The Secret Garden of the Learner at Home', *British Journal of Educational Technology,* 32(2), 233–244

Whichonline (2001) *Annual Internet Survey – The Net Result – Evolution Not Revolution,* Consumer Association
www.which.net/surveys/findings.htm

Whitlock, Q (2000) *Tutor Support in On Line Learning,* Department for Education and Employment

Wood, A (2000) *A Guide to Outreach With Laptops,* NIACE